THE
SAMPLER
MOTIF
BOOK

THE SAMPLER MOTIF BOOK

Brenda Keyes

In needle works there doth great knowledge rest.
A fine conceit thereby full soone is showne:
A drowsie braine this skill cannot digest,
Paine spent on such, in vaine awaie is throne:
They must be careful, diligent and wise,
In needle workes that beare away the prise.

From *A Booke of Curious and Strange
Inventions called the first part of Needleworkes*
published by William Barley in 1596.

THE READER'S DIGEST ASSOCIATION, INC.
Pleasantville, New York/Montreal

For Irene and Jim Keyes,
with grateful thanks and much love

A READER'S DIGEST BOOK

Edited and produced by David & Charles
Designed by Malcolm Couch

Text, designs and charts Copyright © Brenda Keyes 1995
Photography Copyright © David & Charles 1995

All rights reserved. Unauthorized reproduction, in any manner, is prohibited.

First published in the UK 1995

Library of Congress Cataloging in Publication Data
Keyes, Brenda.
    The sampler motif book / Brenda Keyes.
        p.   cm.
    Includes bibliographical references and index.
    ISBN 0-89577-918-8
    1. Cross-stitch—Patterns.   2. Samplers.   I. Title.
TT778.C76K496   1997
746.44'3041—DC20   96-42933

Printed in Italy

Contents

Introduction

The main aim of this book is to show the enormous potential of the sampler as a source of inspiration for needlework design. I have always had an all-consuming passion for samplers, stemming, I feel, from not only their obvious charm but also the wealth of design possibilities contained within those meticulously executed borders. Consider the composition of an "average" sampler (I use the word tentatively, as designs are so diverse), comprising border, alphabets, verse, and spot motifs. Borders range from a simple backstitch line to intricate and complex creations that, in some instances, can stand on their own, maybe needing only a simple verse to complete the design. Alphabets, too, seem to revel in extremes, from the totally uniform understated variety—much in evidence on Quaker samplers—to the wonderfully exuberant floral extravagances beloved by French needlewomen of the 19th century. Verses range from dour warnings of impending death, to sweet sentiment and romanticism, religion, obedience and, occasionally, even humor. This example—"In reading this if any faults you see, Mend them yourself and find no fault in me"—is positive proof, if any were needed, that not all samplers were a labor of love.

Motifs used throughout the ages include an enormous variety of subjects. *The Needle's Excellency* a 17th-century pattern book by John Taylor ("wherein are divers admirable workes wrought with the needle. Newly invented and cut in copper for the pleasure and profit of the industrious"), contains the following verse:

Flowers, Plants and Fishes
Beasts, Birds, Flyes and Bees,
Hills, Dales, Plains, Pastures,
Skies, Seas, Rivers, Trees.
There's nothing ne'er at hand or farthest sought
But with the needle may be shap'd and wrought.

This verse embodies my feelings on the subject admirably!

Some months ago, while happily browsing in a large, dilapidated junk shop (to describe it as an antiques store would, I fear, give it too much dignity), I spotted an extremely moth-eaten, damp-spotted but "promising" sampler right at the very back of the shop. Climbing over several awkwardly placed and lethal-looking antiquities to get to it, I aroused the attention of the owner who, anxious to avoid catastrophe, nimbly leapt over the said antiquities and retrieved it for me.

"Is it the frame you're after, then?" he asked knowledgeably.

"No," I replied, thoroughly taken aback at the notion that my moth-eaten treasure wasn't recognized for the prize it *clearly* was.

"It's actually the rather beautiful sampler that's taking up space in it!"

Thoroughly he was chastened (I like to think) and hoping for a sale (a more likely explanation!), he proceeded to admire and compliment my dust-shrouded "find." I left the store with my sampler carefully wrapped in the finest newspaper, leaving the owner looking extremely puzzled. Perhaps it had something to do with my retreating remark, that not only was my purchase an unusual piece, but much more important than that, it had great potential! Perhaps if he should stumble across this book someday (hopefully not in his store), he will understand.

You will notice that at the end of most of the projects in this book, there is a Variations section. This offering is borne out of sheer frustration—I can always think of many more adaptations and uses for the projects than there would ever be time to stitch and therefore show in the book. These variations are merely suggestions for either adapting the design or taking it one stage further. Hopefully, they will fire your imagination and inspire you to create some wonderful designs of your own. Further inspiration can be found in almost any sampler, old or new. I hope this book may encourage you to take a fresh look at the subject and explore the possibility of using elements of sampler design to create "divers admirable workes" of your own.

Brenda Keyes

Workbox

Most of the projects in this book use the technique of counted cross stitch, where the design is worked from a chart instead of being printed on fabric or canvas. The technique involved in "reading" the chart and then "translating" it to the fabric is an easy one to master and, once understood, will open up a host of exciting possibilities. Not only will you be able to work from any counted cross stitch chart but you will also find it easy to adapt, enlarge, reduce, and eventually create designs of your own easily and quickly.

Understanding Charts

There are many different types of charts—black and white, hand-drawn, computer-generated, colored squares or symbols, or colored squares with symbols. However, if this list sounds complicated and daunting, fear not! The method for

translating all of them is the same. One square on the chart, containing a symbol or color, represents one stitch (usually a cross stitch) on your fabric. Figure 1 and the picture below show clearly how the chart has been "translated" onto the fabric.

The blank squares on your chart mean that this area is unworked (one very good reason, I am sure, for the huge popularity of cross stitch—no unending acres of beige ever-looming in the background to fill in!). The straight black lines surrounding a motif indicate backstitch. They will add impact to your design and will often help to define areas that would otherwise blend into each other. Black is usually suggested for outlining but is sometimes too harsh, in which case a softer shade of gray or brown, or any darker shade of a color already used, is more appropriate. Unless the design is worked in one color only, a key will be given to indicate which colors to use for each stitch.

Figure 1: Chart for Bird in a Bush motif.

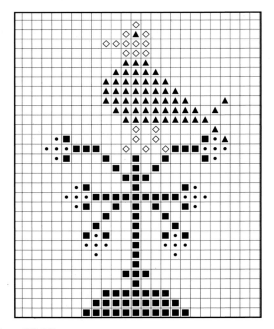

Key DMC

◇	370	Olive green	■	500	Dark green
▲	300	Chocolate brown	•	760	Pink

Bird in a Bush: The finished embroidery.

Threads

The vast selection of threads available to the stitcher today, offered in an enormous choice of colors, means almost unlimited design possibilities. The most commonly used thread for counted cross stitch is six-strand embroidery floss. It is treated by a process known as mercerization, which gives it a polished sheen like silk. The advantage of stranded floss is that the strands can be separated and recombined in any number for different effects. As the floss has six strands, many variations are possible. Two strands are commonly used for cross stitch, although one strand can be used over one thread of fabric to create delicate effects or to give emphasis when outlining in backstitch. One strand over one thread is also used for working long verses on samplers. This effectively reduces the size of the verse by half and eliminates the possibility of swamping the overall design.

There is no reason to limit yourself to the sole use of stranded embroidery floss. Wonderful effects can be achieved by substituting different thread. Try experimenting with threads you may not have used before—pearl cotton, flower thread, metallic thread, fine wool yarn, viscose rayon thread—the list is endless. A somewhat ordinary piece of work can be totally transformed by the substitution or addition of some of the more unusual threads.

Pearl cotton is a highly mercerized, twisted, nondivisible, lustrous cotton thread available in a skein or a ball. Crewel wool is a fine, smooth, 2-ply yarn. Flower thread is a nondivisible, matte-finish thread made of 100 percent cotton. Marlitt is a 4-ply, viscose rayon thread with a high sheen. The projects in this book use DMC stranded embroidery floss unless otherwise specified. There is a DMC to Anchor conversion chart on page 124 for those who wish to use Anchor threads. All pearl cottons used are No. 5.

Using Space-dyed or Variegated Thread

Wonderful effects can be achieved if these threads are used sympathetically. A simple design (a sampler motif, for example) can be transformed by substituting this type of thread for a single color. When using variegated thread (where the color gradually changes from a very pale to a dark shade of the same color), it is important to select the lengths so that the gradual change of color is followed throughout your stitching, that is, do not place dark thread next to light. Beautifully subtle effects can be achieved if the colors merge gradually. On the other hand, some space-dyed

threads are dyed with sudden and dramatic changes of color at short intervals, giving a totally different look. For both types of thread, it is important to complete each cross individually, and not work a line of half crosses and then complete by working back along the line.

Thread Storage

Storing your threads in an organized and efficient manner will allow you to see and select threads at a glance. There are many methods of thread storage, ranging from cards with holes punched in them to hold cut skeins, storage boxes with cards to wrap threads around, and sophisticated thread organizers that store threads in plastic pockets which are then housed in a binder. Whichever method you choose (including your own versions of the above), storing your threads carefully will mean that they are clean, tangle-free, and freely available for selection.

Needles

You will need blunt tapestry needles for all types of counted needlework. The most commonly used sizes are 22, 24, and 26. The size selected will depend on the fabric used, for example, size 22 for 8-count Aida, size 26 for fine 30- to 36-count linen. The needle should offer a little pressure when passed through the fabric and should not be able to drop right through the hole. Special long, fine needles are available for beading. Always try to keep an assortment of needles in stock, as it is infuriating not to be able to start a project for the lack of the appropriate needle.

Fabrics

Counted needlework requires an evenweave fabric, that is, a fabric that has the same number of threads vertically as horizontally. Such fabrics are described by the number of threads or blocks per inch, usually known as the count. This count will determine the finished size of the design. A wonderful variety of evenweave fabrics is now available for counted needlework, with two main types—Aida and linen. Aida fabrics are constructed in blocks, which makes counting easier and prevents uneven stitching, especially for beginners.

Various types of Aida and linen fabrics have been used for the projects in this book. Aida fabrics include: Ainring, which is woven to form blocks of four threads, with 18 blocks to the inch; Rustico, available in 14- or 18-count, which is a naturally woven cotton fabric with a country feel; Hardanger, which is a cotton fabric woven with pairs of threads, usually 22 pairs to the inch.

Linen fabrics include: Edinburgh linen, a 36-count, high-quality linen; Belfast linen, of similar quality, but in 32-count; Dublin linen, a 25-count linen woven from fine-quality flax; and Cork linen, a 19-count linen, made from strong bleached flax.

Aida, linen, and even perforated paper (much loved by the Victorians) are available in a wide choice of colors. Do try experimenting—you need not restrict yourself to white, beige, or cream. Working your design on a colored background will bring a different dimension to your work instantly. You could even try dyeing your own fabrics with one of the commercial fabric dyes, or really go back to basics and research methods of dyeing fabrics with natural dyes such as madder or indigo (or the more readily available onion skins).

Fabric Allowance

It is essential to allow enough fabric surrounding the design area for stretching and framing. As a general rule, 4–6 in (10–15 cm) will be adequate, although smaller pieces, such as brooches, miniatures, and cards, will not need this much excess. The following information shows how to calculate the amount of fabric required for a design (or alternative fabrics with different thread counts). Once you have mastered the technique of calculating this way, you will find it an easy task to select the correct amount of fabric required for counted work. Always measure your fabric carefully and cut along a thread line using sharp dressmaking scissors. There are a number of methods you can use to prevent the cloth from fraying: overcast the edges by hand; machine-stitch the edges using a zigzag stitch; bind the edges with tape (not masking tape, which can pull threads being removed and can also leave a nasty sticky residue); or use a commercially made liquid fray preventer, which is applied to the edges of the fabric to seal them.

Calculating Quantities of Alternative Fabrics

Cross Stitching on Linen over Two Threads

For example: 25 threads per inch linen with design area 100 stitches x 50 wide. Divide the number of vertical stitches in the design area by the thread count of the fabric and multiply by 2. This will give you the size of the design area in inches. Repeat this procedure for the horizontal stitches.

Thus:

$$\frac{100}{25} = 4 \times 2 = 8 \text{ in } (20.5 \text{ cm})$$

$$\frac{50}{25} = 2 \times 2 = 4 \text{ in } (10 \text{ cm})$$

So the design area is 4 x 8 in (10 x 20.5 cm).

Add 4–6 in (10–15 cm) for finishing, and the fabric required is 8 x 12 in (20.5 x 30.5 cm).

Cross Stitching on Block Fabrics, such as Aida, or over one Thread of Linen

For example: 10-count Aida with design area 100 stitches high x 50 wide. Divide the number of vertical stitches in the design area by the thread count of the fabric, and this will give you the design area in inches. Repeat this procedure for the horizontal stitches.

Thus:

$$\frac{100}{10} = 10 \text{ in } (25.5 \text{ cm})$$

$$\frac{50}{10} = 5 \text{ in } (12.5 \text{ cm})$$

So the design area is 5 x 10 in (12.5 x 25.5 cm).

Add 4–6 in (10–15 cm) for finishing, and the fabric required is 9 x 14 in (23 x 35 cm).

Hoops and Frames

If you decide to use an embroidery hoop—and they can be a very helpful aid to accurate stitching—always use one that is big enough to house the complete design comfortably. This will ensure that the hoop never needs to be placed over any stitching and will thus avoid spoiling the completed work with pulled and snagged stitches. To prevent your fabric from slipping, it is advisable to bind the inner hoop with white cotton binding tape secured with a few stitches.

Another way to protect your work from hoop marks is to place a piece of tissue paper between the fabric and hoop, then tear away the middle section to expose the area to be worked. Hoops tend to leave crease marks that are almost impossible to remove, so always remember to remove the hoop every time you finish working.

Larger pieces of work will need a rectangular roller frame. They come in many sizes, including large freestanding floor frames. Some have the added benefit of a magnifier and light. After the side edges of the fabric have been bound with tape or hemmed to strengthen them, the top and bottom edges of the fabric are sewn to the webbing, which is attached to the rollers of the frame. It is important to make sure that the fabric is placed evenly in the frame; if it is sewn in unevenly, it will become distorted. The frame is then assembled and the side edges laced to the stretchers with very long thread (see Figure 2).

A quicker and easier, though just as effective, way of keeping your fabric taut is to use ready-made rectangular frames, which are available in a variety of sizes from some embroidery or artists' suppliers. The fabric is stapled straight onto the frame (or attached with thumbtacks), thus saving a great deal of time and effort. Although less

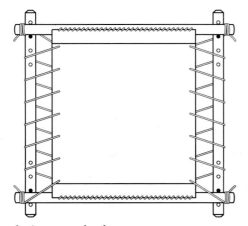

Figure 2: A rectangular frame.

elegant than roller frames, they have many advantages—there are no protruding corners to catch your thread on, they are lighter to hold, easier to store, and more portable. For really large pieces of work, however, where the overall size would rule out the possibility of holding the entire framed piece comfortably, a roller frame would be more appropriate.

Adhesives

For some of the projects you will need to use glue, for example, to glue a piece of embroidery in a fold-over card. There are many adhesives available, but I often prefer to use instant-bonding glue, which is recommended for use with fabric and dries on contact. White craft glue is a suitable alternative in many of the projects and is useful if you want to be able to move the piece slightly before the glue dries.

Enlarging and Reducing Designs

Charted designs are extremely versatile and very easy to enlarge or reduce in size. There are a number of ways to do this.

1 Consider every square in the design to be two, three, or even four stitches square instead of one. For example, to triple the design size, work a block of stitches three by three for every single stitch shown on the chart.

2 Work the stitches over two, three, or even four threads or blocks of fabric (Aida commonly). For example, if you work over four threads instead of two, the design will double in size. Likewise, if the instructions state that the design is worked in cross stitch over two threads of linen and you work over just one thread in either cross stitch or tent stitch, the design size will be halved.

3 The fabric chosen will also play a large part in determining the size of the design. For example, working over one block of 11-count Aida as opposed to working the same design over one thread of linen 36 threads per inch will increase the design size dramatically.

By using any of the methods described here, you will be able to make much more use of the motifs, alphabets, and borders shown in this book. For example, the repeated strawberry motif used for the pincushion on page 99 is worked over just one thread of fine canvas in a fine crewel wool. Worked in tapestry yarn on a larger-gauge canvas over two threads in cross stitch, it would easily translate into a pillow. Likewise, any of the larger motifs worked over two threads could be worked over one on a fine linen and used for brooches, bookmarks, or miniatures, etc.

How to Begin Working

Finding the Center of the Fabric

Fold your fabric in half in both directions and crease lightly. Baste along these lines in a contrasting sewing thread. The center of the fabric is where the lines cross. Most instructions suggest that you begin work at this point—this helps you make sure that your work is distributed evenly, avoiding the horrible possibility of working off the edge of the fabric. However, if you want to start work at, say, the top left-hand corner of the design (and this does seem to be a more logical alternative with designs that include a border), you must carefully calculate where to start by deducting the design size from your fabric size and positioning accordingly. For example, if your fabric size is 10 x 12 in (25.5 x 30.5 cm) and your design size 6 x 8 in (15 x 20.5 cm), you will have 4 in (10 cm) of spare fabric. You should therefore measure 2 in (5 cm) down from the top edge and 2 in (5 cm) from the side edge and begin work here.

Starting to Stitch

The following list of dos and don'ts will help you achieve a perfect start and a perfect finish.

1 Cut your thread no longer than 12–18 in (30.5–45.5 cm).

2 When using embroidery floss always separate and untwist all six strands before selecting the number of strands required. (The amount will depend on the fabric used.) This method will help the threads to lie flatter and will give greater coverage.

3 Never use a knot to begin stitching. Knots can pull through the fabric and will give a bumpy finish that will spoil the appearance of your work. To begin stitching previously unworked fabric, bring the needle up through the fabric, leaving about an inch of thread at the back. Holding this thread in place, work three or four stitches until the trailing thread is caught and secured. To begin a new thread on fabric that has been previously stitched, simply run the needle through the loops of three or four stitches at the back of the work near to where you wish to begin stitching. Bring the needle up at the required place and begin.

4 Be careful not to pull stitches too tightly. They should sit evenly on the fabric—tension is just as important in embroidery as in knitting.

5 Make sure that all top stitches in cross stitch are worked in the same direction to give a smooth, even finish.

6 Remember to "drop" your needle every four to five stitches. This will take the twist out of the thread and avoid tangles.

7 The method for finishing and securing a thread is much the same as starting. Leaving yourself enough thread to finish, take the needle through to the back of the work. Run the needle through the back loop of three or four stitches and cut off the thread close to the stitching.

Working the Project

Stitch instructions are given in the Stitch Directory on page 122. Further skills, such as finishing, mounting, and framing a completed piece of embroidery, making a fold-over card, or a twisted cord and tassels, are described at the back of the book (see Finishing Techniques, pages 118–122).

Band Sampler

The 17th century has been described as the "Golden Age of the Sampler." Many early samplers were real works of art, often more than a yard long. They were rolled on a small ivory rod, made for the purpose of storage. This example is worked in cross stitch and backstitch on linen, and although it is not as long and narrow as early examples, the sampler features many of the border patterns and alphabets that could have appeared on them.

Design size: $9\frac{1}{4}$ x $12\frac{1}{4}$ in (23.5 x 31 cm)
Stitch count: 115 x 154

13 x 16 in (33 x 40.5 cm) natural Dublin linen, 25 threads per inch (2.5 cm)
Embroidery floss as shown in the key

Use 2 strands of floss over 2 threads of linen, except for the verse, remaining words, and date, which are worked over 1 thread of linen.

1 Find the center of the design and work out from this point following the chart.

2 Using the main chart on pages 16–17, first work the main body of the design in cross stitch and backstitch over two threads of linen. To add the verse, words, and date, use the main chart to position the first letter on each line and then follow the additional chart (below), working over just one thread of linen.

3 Substitute your name and date using the alphabets in the chart on pages 16–17. Chart the details on graph paper and position as shown.

4 Stretch, mount, and frame as desired (see pages 118 –122).

VARIATIONS
■ Add more borders and alphabets from the book to make a longer band sampler.

■ Use any of the borders to decorate household linen. The backstitch border would look stunning worked in black on white table napkins.

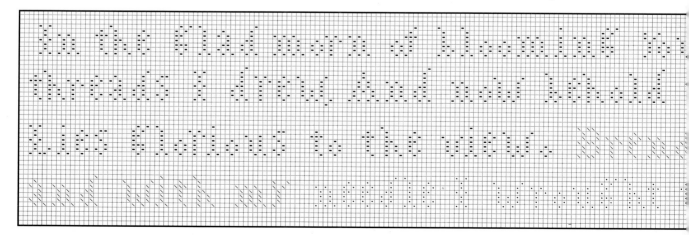

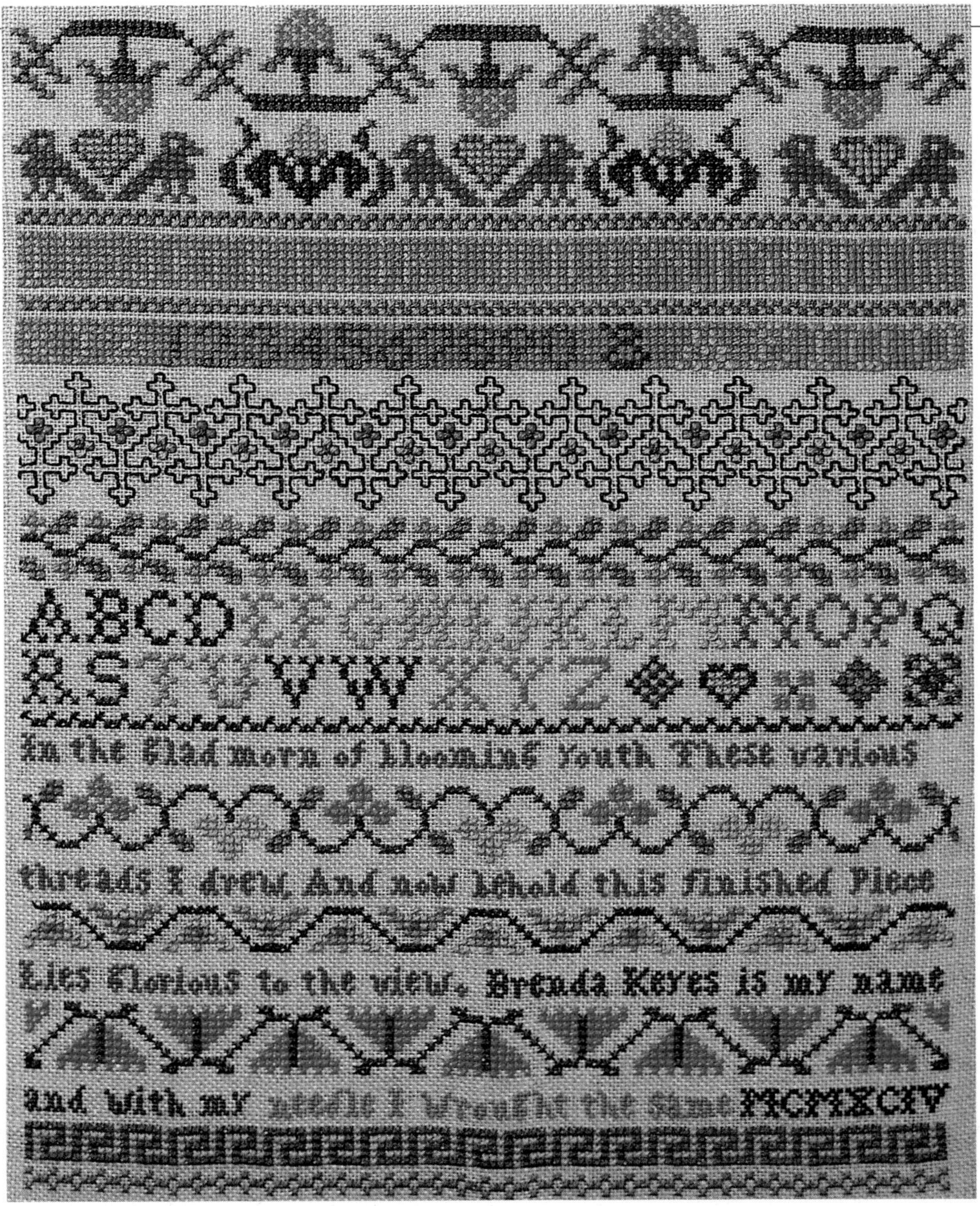

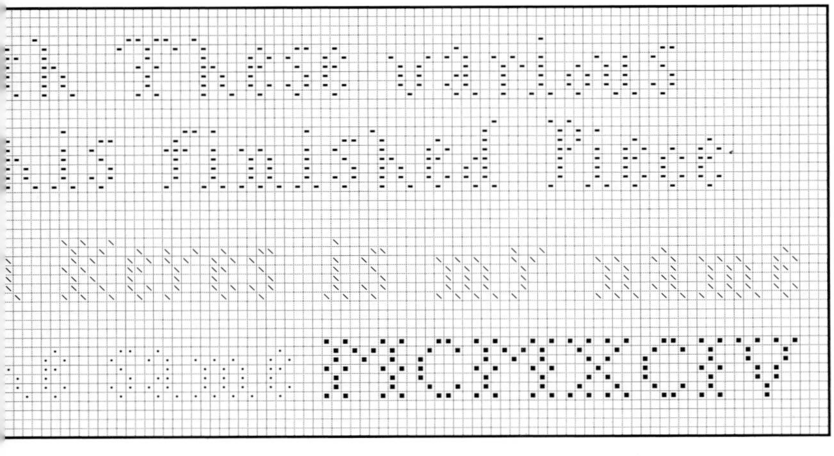

Band Sampler Lettering

Key	DMC	
[symbol]	300	Chocolate brown
[symbol]	890	Dark green
[symbol]	434	Warm brown
[symbol]	3371	Very dark brown

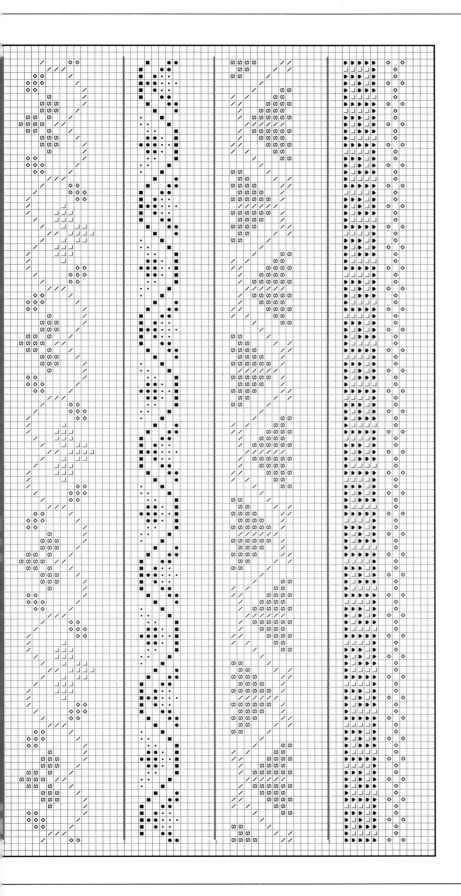

Work backstitch in 3371 Very dark brown.
See additional chart on pages 14–15
for verse/name, etc., and insert where
indicated by the red lines.

Band Sampler

Key DMC

890	Dark green	
732	Sage green	
347	Dull red	
680	Dark gold	
300	Chocolate brown	

413	Dark gray	
926	Light slate blue	
3371	Very dark brown	
434	Warm brown	

Bush with Repeat Pattern Border

The addition of an elaborate and subtly shaded border transforms this simple motif of a bush into a most unusual piece. It is worked in cross stitch on evenweave fabric.

Design size: 5 x 5 in (12.5 x 12.5 cm)
Stitch count: 81 x 81

9 x 9 in (23 x 23 cm) natural Floba linen, 18 threads per inch (2.5 cm)
Embroidery floss as shown in the key

Use 2 strands of floss over 1 thread of fabric.

1 Find the center of the design and work out from this point following the chart.

2 Stretch, mount, and frame as desired (see pages 118–122).

VARIATIONS

■ Substitute bright primary colors for those used in the border, and use the design as a basis for a birth sampler. Add the child's name, date of birth, etc., using the additional alphabets on pages 114–115 and working out your details in pencil on graph paper.

■ Substitute any other sampler motif of a suitable size from the book for the center panel.

■ Work the border design in cross stitch with yarn on canvas to make a belt. Repeat the pattern for the required length.

Detail of repeat pattern border.

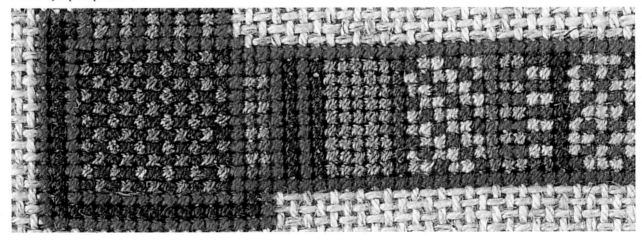

Bush with Repeat Pattern Border

Key	DMC						
	355	Dark rust		597	Soft turquoise	957	Bright pink
	924	Antique blue		434	Warm brown	422	Light gold
	3041	Mauve		3371	Very dark brown	926	Light slate blue
				315	Plum	730	Sage green

Bookmarks

This simple but effective idea uses small pieces of perforated paper and ribbon or bias binding. Worked in cross stitch, a bookmark would be the perfect addition to give with a book to make the gift really special. Choose any of the designs shown here, or indeed any motif from the book. Tailor the design either to the book itself—for example, the bunch of grapes for a book on wine—the ABC for a child's book, etc., or work the recipient's initials using an alphabet from the book.

Bookmarks
Small pieces of perforated paper (the exact size depends on your chosen design)

Embroidery floss as shown in the key
Ribbon or bias binding
Craft glue/contact adhesive

Use 2 strands of floss over 1 block of perforated paper.

1 Choose your design, then count the number of squares vertically and horizontally to assess the size of perforated paper needed. Cut two pieces the same size, allowing for trimming and gluing the corner edges together.

2 Find the center of the design and match it to the center of one piece of perforated paper. Work from this point following the chart.

3 Cut two pieces of contrasting ribbon or bias binding the same length as the right-hand corner edges and apply a little glue to the wrong side of each piece. Place the unworked piece of perforated paper on the back of the worked piece, matching the holes. Fold each piece of glued ribbon in turn lengthwise onto one of the corner edges and press into place.

4 Trim any rough edges, or cut into a shape if you wish (see photo on page 21).

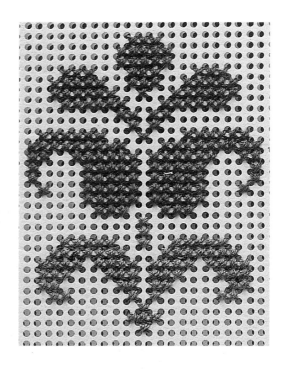

VARIATIONS

■ To make an "heirloom" bookmark, work a complex design (an ecclesiastical design for a family Bible, for example) over one thread of fine linen. Finish as described, but fold the outer edges under and line with parchment paper.

■ Use any of the motifs shown here to decorate a small trinket box lid.

■ Work one of the motifs on a longer piece of perforated paper to make a larger bookmark.

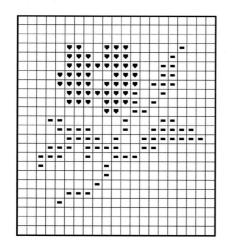
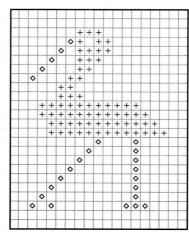
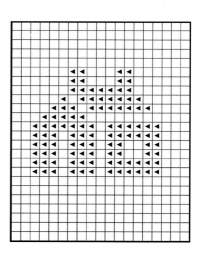

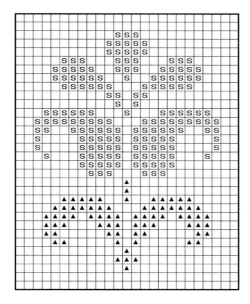
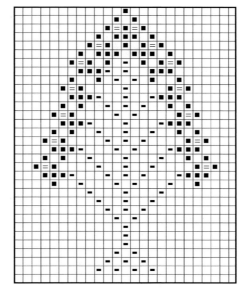

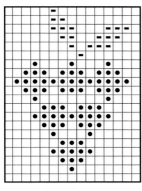
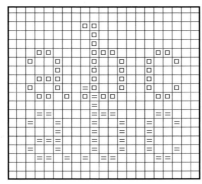
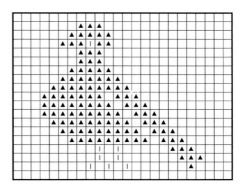

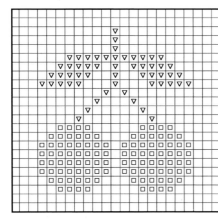
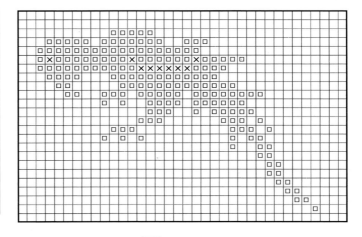

Bookmarks

Key	DMC					
321	Red	327	Dark purple	+ +	Ecru	
444	Bright yellow	D282	Gold thread	3371	Very dark brown	
552	Purple	315	Plum	356	Apricot	
730	Sage green	3768	Blue	823	Navy	
		3378	Pale apricot	890	Dark green	

23

Cherub Card and Picture

Cherub motifs can be found in many of the sampler designs of the past. They were particularly beloved by the Victorians, who seemed to revel in romance and sentimentality. "Nothing wrong with that," I say, and judging by the huge popularity of all things Victorian over the last decade, I am not alone. The picture and card are worked in cross stitch on linen.

The Picture
Design size: 2 x 4³/₄ in (5 x 12 cm)
Stitch count: 30 x 71

5 x 7 in (12.5 x 18 cm) cream Belfast linen,
32 threads per inch (2.5 cm)
Embroidery floss as shown in the key
Frame

Use 2 strands of floss over 2 threads of linen for the cherub motif, and 1 strand over 1 thread of linen for the initial.

THE PICTURE

1 Find the center of the design and work out from this point following the chart.

2 Choose your initial from the alphabet shown on page 96, and center it within the heart by counting the number of squares horizontally and vertically on the chart and matching the midpoint of the initial to the midpoint of the heart. (Note: The initial is worked over only one thread of linen.)

3 Stretch, mount, and frame as desired (see pages 118–122).

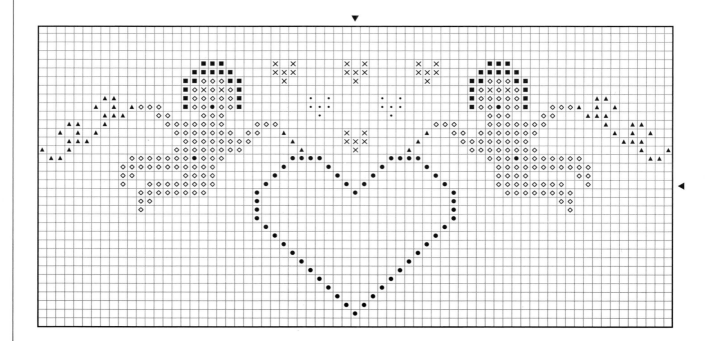

24

The Card
Design size: 2 x 3 1/8 in (5 x 8 cm)
Stitch count: 30 x 47

4 x 5 in (10 x 12.5 cm) cream Belfast linen, 32
threads per inch (2.5 cm)
Embroidery floss as shown in the key
Purchased card

Use 2 strands of floss over 2 threads of linen for
the cherub motif, and 1 strand over 1 thread of
linen for the initial.

Cherub Card and Picture
Key   DMC

○○	842	Flesh	✕✕	927 Pale slate blue
■■	434	Warm brown	▲▲	926 Light slate blue
∴∴	223	Deep pink	∴∴	818 Very light pink

THE CARD

1 Follow steps 1 and 2 on page 24, relocating
center (you do not stitch cherub on right).

2 Insert into the card following the instructions
given on pages 120–121.

VARIATIONS
■ Work the design in cross stitch with yarn on
large-mesh canvas to make a wonderfully roman-
tic Victorian pillow. Edge with cream lace and add
ribbon bows.

■ You could use the design to decorate the lid of a
trinket box.

■ Enlarge the heart and transform the design into
a baby announcement by adding the baby's name,
date of birth, weight, etc., using a small backstitch
alphabet (see page 114).

Birds and Carnations

The intricate balance of this design, with its oversized birds and some remarkably small ones nestling in the foliage, makes for perfect symmetry. No regard whatsoever is given to scale, lending this design a charming naiveté typical of samplers in general. The picture is worked in tent stitch on linen, and the pillow is worked in cross stitch on evenweave fabric.

The Picture
Design size: $5^3/_4 \times 6^3/_4$ in (14.5 x 17 cm)
Stitch count: 100 x 131

$9^1/_2 \times 10^1/_2$ in (24 x 26.5 cm) cream Cork linen, 19 threads per inch (2.5 cm)
Embroidery floss as shown in the key

Use 3 strands of floss over 1 thread of linen.

The Pillow
Design size: $12 \times 15^1/_2$ in (30.5 x 39.5 cm)
Stitch count: 100 x 131

17×17 in (43 x 43 cm) natural Floba linen, 18 threads per inch (2.5 cm)
Embroidery floss as shown in the key
17×17 in (43 x 43 cm) cotton backing fabric
Matching sewing thread
10 in (25.5 cm) zipper (optional)
Pillow form, 16 in (40.5 cm) square
60 in (152.5 cm) length of braided yarn or twisted cord in matching shade

Use 4 strands of floss over 2 threads of fabric.

THE PICTURE

1 Find the center of the design and, using tent stitch (see page 123), work out from this point following the chart. As tent stitch tends to distort fabric, using a frame is advised.

2 Stretch, mount, and frame as desired (see pages 118–122).

Using Tent Stitch
This method of stitching tent stitch over one thread of linen has much to recommend it and can be applied to other charted designs. The advantages of working in this way are that the design is completed in half the time, and, unlike working on canvas, the background does not have to be covered.

The size of the finished design will obviously have to be taken into consideration; usually this method is employed to reduce the size of a design. If you use a larger mesh linen, however, such as Cork with 19 threads per inch (2.5 cm), this will not only produce a finished size that is comparable to 18-count Aida but will also lessen the possibility of eyestrain, which can occur when working on fine linen.

THE PILLOW

1 Find the center of the design, match to the center of the fabric, and, using tent stitch (see page 123), work out from this point using the chart.

2 Pin and baste the embroidery and backing fabric right sides together. Machine- or hand-stitch, leaving an opening large enough on the bottom edge to insert the pillow form. Overcast or zigzag the seams to strengthen them.

3 If you have chosen to insert a zipper, add it at this stage. Alternatively, simply turn the pillow right side out, insert the pillow form, and close the opening with small invisible stitches.

4 Hand-sew the braided yarn or twisted cord to the edge of the pillow, where the embroidery and backing fabric meet, using a matching thread.

VARIATIONS

■ Work the design in yarn on canvas and make it into a pillow or fire screen.

■ Use the design to decorate the lid of a needle-work box.

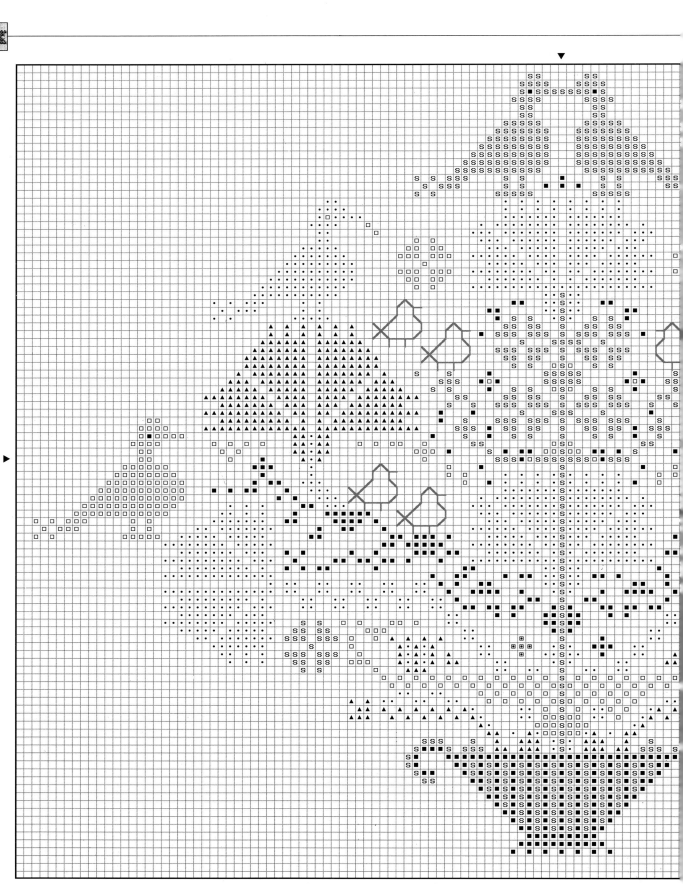

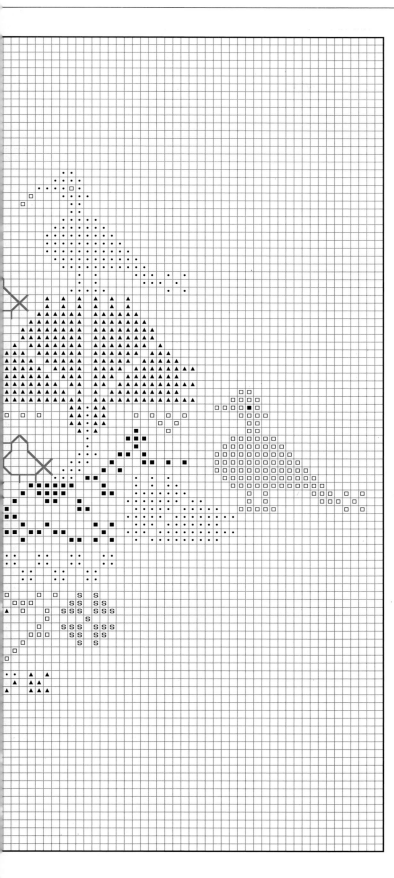

Birds and Carnations

Key   DMC

S S / S S	356	Apricot	
· · / · ·	926	Light slate blue	
□ □ / □ □	355	Dark rust	
▲ ▲ / ▲ ▲	407	Pink-beige	
■ ■ / ■ ■	924	Antique blue	

Work top backstitch birds in 924
Antique blue and bottom backstitch
birds in 355 Dark rust.

Nursery Picture

*"Pretty as a picture" sums up this pastel piece (see page 32) perfectly.
I have deliberately chosen to go "over the top" with the framing of these simple
nursery motifs and a small backstitch alphabet to show that even a simple
piece of embroidery can be totally transformed if careful thought
and imagination are given to finishing. Worked in cross stitch and backstitch
on Aida fabric, this nursery delight is simplicity itself to make.*

*Design size: $2^3/_4$ x 6 in (7 x 15 cm)
Size of finished picture with mat: 13 x 13 in
(33 x 33 cm)
Stitch count: 36 x 81*

*6 x 9 in (15 x 23 cm) pale blue 14-count Aida
6 x 9 in (15 x 23 cm) pale yellow 14-count Aida
Embroidery floss as shown in the key
2 pieces of cardboard 13 x 13 in (33 x 33 cm)
14 x 14 in (35.5 x 35.5 cm) pink and white striped
cotton fabric
2 pieces of cardboard 4 x $7^1/_2$ in (10 x 19 cm)
Craft glue or masking tape
45 in (114.5 cm) narrow pale pink ribbon with a
picot edge
14 x 14 in (35.5 x 35.5 cm) pink cotton fabric
46 in (117 cm) pale pink cotton lace, 1 in (2.5 cm)
wide
18 in (45.5 cm) each of pale pink, rose pink, and green
narrow ribbons
Ready-made deep pink ribbon rose
Frame*

Use 2 strands of floss over 1 block of fabric.

1 For both panels, find the center of the design and work out from this point following the charts.

2 Cut two openings measuring 3 x $6^1/_4$ in (7.5 x 16 cm) in one of the larger pieces of cardboard, positioning the top one $2^3/_4$ in (7cm) from the top edge and centered widthwise, and the second centered $1^1/_4$ in (3 cm) from the bottom of the first opening. Cover with the pink and white striped fabric (see page 119).

3 After lacing each piece of embroidery onto a small piece of cardboard (see page 118), position the covered mat with the two openings carefully on top of the two finished pieces and glue together or attach with masking tape.

4 Cut the pale pink ribbon with the picot edge in two, and glue around the edge of each opening, folding the ribbon at the corners as shown in the photograph.

5 Cut an opening $10^3/_4$ x $10^3/_4$ in (27.5 x 27.5 cm) centered, in the remaining piece of cardboard, and cover with the pink fabric. Glue the pink lace just behind the edge of this covered mat, folding at the corners as shown in the photograph. Position carefully on top of the striped mat and glue together or attach with masking tape.

6 Make eight ribbon bows from the narrow pink and green ribbons (two of each color, and each slightly smaller than the one before), and sew together. Sew the ribbon rose in the center of the bows to cover the stitching and then glue into place at the top left-hand corner as shown in the photograph. The work is now ready for framing.

7 Frame as desired (see page 120). I used a plain unvarnished pine frame, painted first with pale blue-green stencil paint and then "dragged" with strawberry pink paint. You need no

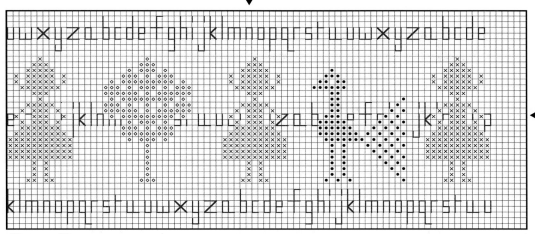

Nursery Picture

Key   DMC

316   Deep pink

954   Light green

597   Soft turquoise

Top and bottom backstitch alphabets 356 Apricot

Middle alphabet Ecru

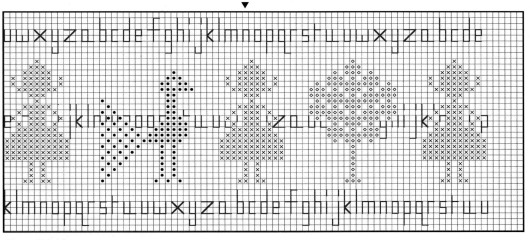

Key   DMC

316   Deep pink

597   Soft turquoise

954   Light green

Top and bottom alphabets 827 Pale blue

Middle alphabet 356 Apricot

special talent for painting to achieve this effect since it is meant to look irregular.

VARIATIONS

■ See the nursery pictures following (pages 33–35).

■ Use the border design to decorate a towel. You could use a purchased one with an Aida insert, or work on an Aida band and stitch it to an ordinary towel.

■ Use the design to decorate a baby's bib.

■ Work the border design on an Aida or linen band and stitch it to the edge of sheets or pillowcases for the nursery.

■ Replace the alphabet with a child's name and date of birth to transform the piece into a birth sampler.

Overleaf: Nursery Picture and Nursery Triplets.

Nursery Triplets

These three charming pastel miniatures, based on the Nursery Picture on page 30, worked in cross stitch and backstitch on Aida fabric, will add the perfect touch to a nursery.

Design size: $1^{7}/_{8}$ x $2^{1}/_{2}$ in (4.5 x 6.5 cm)
Size of picture with mat: $4^{1}/_{2}$ x $4^{1}/_{2}$ in
(11.5 x 11.5 cm)
Stitch count: 26 x 34

To make the set of three
4 x 4 in (10 x 10 cm) 14-count Aida fabric in each of pale yellow, pale pink, and pale blue
Embroidery floss as shown in the key
3 pieces of cardboard $4^{1}/_{2}$ x $4^{1}/_{2}$ in (11.5 x 11.5 cm)
$5^{1}/_{2}$ x $16^{1}/_{2}$ in (14 x 42 cm) cream cotton fabric, cut into 3 pieces $5^{1}/_{2}$ x $5^{1}/_{2}$ in (14 x 14 cm)

3 pieces of cardboard 3 x $3^{1}/_{2}$ in (7.5 x 9 cm)
Glue or masking tape
12 deep pink shirt buttons
18 in (45.5 cm) each of rose pink and pale blue narrow ribbons
3 ready-made deep mauve ribbon roses
3 plain wooden frames to fit a $4^{1}/_{2}$ x $4^{1}/_{2}$ in (11.5 x 11.5 cm) mat

Use 2 strands of floss over 1 block of fabric.

1 For each picture, find the center of the design and work out from this point following the chart.

2 Cut an opening measuring $2^{1}/_{4}$ x $2^{3}/_{4}$ in (5.5 x 7 cm) centered in each of the larger pieces of cardboard and cover with cream cotton fabric (see page 119).

3 After lacing the embroidery pieces onto a small piece of cardboard (see page 118), place the covered mats carefully on top of the finished pieces and glue together or attach with tape.

4 Glue a shirt button face down, so that the flat side is uppermost, at each corner of the cream-covered mat, as shown in the photograph on the facing page.

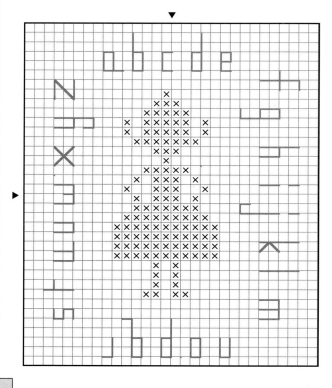

Pink
Key		DMC	
×× ××		316	Mauve
letters		597	Soft turquoise

Blue
×× ××		316	Mauve
letters		745	Soft yellow

Yellow
×× ××		316	Mauve
letters		954	Pale green

The pink project. All three can be seen on page 33.

5 Make tiny ribbon bows from the pink and blue ribbons (one of each color for each embroidered piece) and sew together. Sew a ribbon rose to the center of the bows to cover the stitching and, after assembling the embroidery in the frame, glue in place as shown above. (See page 30 for painting a frame.)

VARIATIONS

■ Replace the alphabet with a child's name repeated around the edge.

■ Work the design on the pocket of a blouse using waste canvas (see page 122).

■ Work the design in bright primary colors and paint a frame to match.

Home Sweet Home

The Home Sweet Home sampler
has retained its popularity since
Victorian times. Worked in cross
stitch on linen using only five colors
of floss, this particular version
will look equally at home in
an old or new house.

Design size: $10^{1}/_{2}$ x $10^{3}/_{4}$ in (26.5 x 27.5 cm)
Stitch count: 135 x 135

$14^{1}/_{2}$ x $14^{1}/_{2}$ in (37 x 37 cm) cream Dublin linen,
25 threads per inch (2.5 cm)
Embroidery floss as shown in the key

Use 2 strands of floss over 2 threads of linen.

1 Find the center of the design and work out
from this point following the chart.

2 Stretch, mount, and frame as desired (see
pages 118–122).

VARIATIONS

■ Make the design as a pillow with muslin backing and pipe in blue.

■ Substitute the name of your house, or house
number and name of your street, or a favorite
verse or saying for the words "Home Sweet
Home."

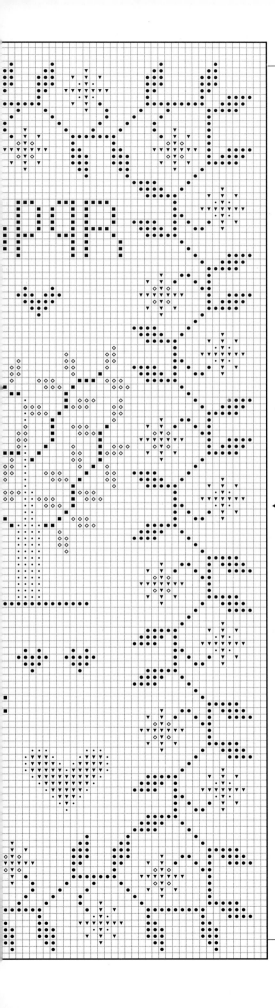

Home Sweet Home

Key DMC

■ ■	3371	Very dark brown
· ·	434	Warm brown
◇ ◇	926	Light slate blue
▼ ▼	738	Light beige
● ●	924	Antique blue
△ △	One strand 3371 and one strand 926	

Sampler Motif Guitar Strap

Of all the many needlework gifts I have made for family and friends over the years, those that seem to have brought the most pleasure are the decorative guitar/banjo straps I have made for musician friends. Worked in cross stitch on a natural linen band in subtle sampler shades, this highly unusual, yet simple-to-make guitar strap will bring delight to any budding musician.

Design size: 3 x 39 in (7.5 x 99 cm) (Adjust length to suit player—choose one or more of the motifs from the chart to add length to the design)

2 lengths of natural linen band, 3 in (7.5 cm) wide x required length, plus 2 in (5 cm) for finishing
Embroidery floss as shown in the key
Matching sewing thread
2 leather guitar strap ends removed from purchased strap (these are inexpensive and readily available from most music stores)

Use 2 strands of floss over 2 threads of natural linen band.

1 Measure $2^{1}/_2$ in (6.5 cm) from the top of the linen band and begin working the two birds that are facing each other here.

2 To substitute the recipient's initials for those shown, use an alphabet chart from pages 114–115, and chart the chosen initials in pencil on graph paper. Position as shown in the chart.

3 When you have worked enough motifs to complete the desired length, pin, baste, and then overcast the side edges of the unworked

length of linen band to the wrong side of the worked length in matching sewing thread, using small stitches. Leave the short ends open.

4 Insert the guitar strap ends, then fold the linen band in at the sides to fit. Turn under $^{1}/_2$ in (1.5 cm) at each bottom edge, enclosing the guitar strap ends, and overcast together. Finally, backstitch through all thicknesses at each end, just above the guitar strap end, to keep them flat.

VARIATIONS
■ Work on linen and widen the design by repeating the motifs. Back with fabric to make a charming bell pull.

■ Use this design, or a combination of any of the smaller motifs in the book, to decorate a belt or pair of suspenders.

■ Use any of the motifs individually to make unique greeting cards.

■ Shorten the length of the design and use for a glasses case.

■ Use the motifs to decorate a height chart for a child (numerals can be found on pages 114–115).

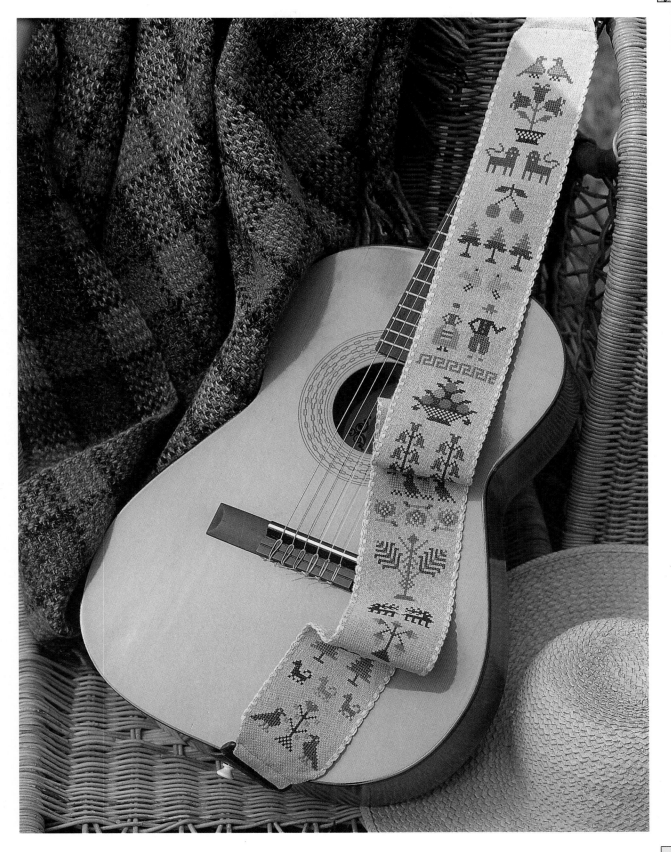

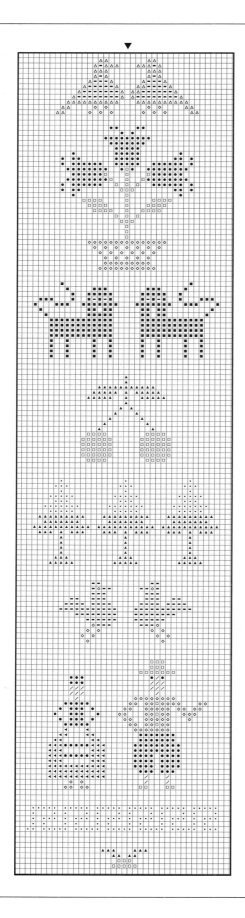

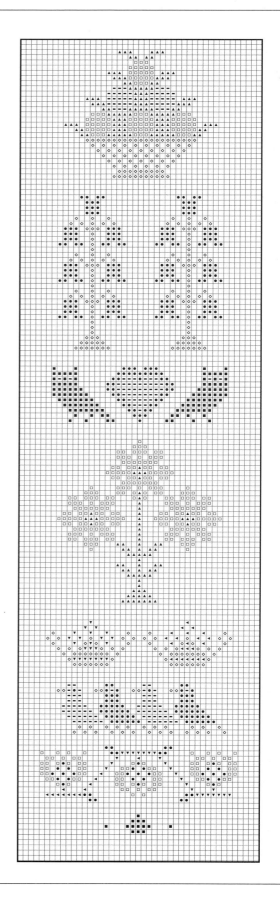

Sampler Motif Guitar Strap

Key	DMC	
△△ △△	918	Medium rust
━┃━ ━┃━	680	Dark gold
◇◇ ◇◇	3371	Very dark brown
●● ●●	924	Antique blue
□□ □□	355	Dark rust
■■ ■■	300	Chocolate brown
▲▲ ▲▲	890	Dark green
∙∙ ∙∙	732	Dark sage
╱╱ ╱╱	407	Pink-beige
◀◀ ◀◀	921	Light rust

Alphabet Sampler

Try encouraging a young member of the family to take up cross stitch by working this simple alphabet sampler. Ideal as a practice piece—girls as young as five years of age would have made similar pieces in the past—this charming little sampler would provide a perfect introduction to stitching. A beginner could substitute 14-count Aida fabric for the linen.

Design size: $4^1/_2$ x $6^3/_4$ in (11.5 x 17 cm)
Stitch count: 62 x 95

8 x 10 in (20.5 x 25.5 cm) unbleached linen,
28 threads per inch (2.5 cm)
Embroidery floss as shown in the key

Use 2 strands of floss over 2 threads of linen.

1   Find the center of the design and work out from this point following the chart.

2   Chart your name from the alphabets given and the date from the backstitch numerals on page 114. Chart your details on graph paper in pencil and position as shown.

3   Stretch, mount, and frame as desired (see pages 118 –122).

VARIATIONS

- Work in pastel colors on cream linen for a birth sampler, adding an extra line at the bottom of the design for the date of birth.

■ Add a border to make a larger sampler.

■ Use the letters to personalize any appropriate cross stitch design by adding your name.

Alphabet Sampler Key DMC

	823	Navy
	729	Gold
	355	Dark rust
	732	Dark sage
	890	Dark green

Carnation Pillow

This bold needlepoint pillow with its repeated carnation motif and tulip border is worked in tent stitch with subtle shades of yarn on canvas. The carnation and the tulip—both much-loved designs—were frequently used throughout the last four centuries as both border and single motifs. Symbolically, this pillow represents love, as the tulip is often associated with perfect love and the carnation with maternal love. (See pages 116–117 for more symbolic meanings of motifs.)

Design size: 13¹/₂ x 14¹/₂ in (34.5 x 37 cm)
Stitch count: 137 x 149

18 x 18 in (45.5 x 45.5 cm) white interlock canvas, 10 holes per inch (2.5 cm)
DMC Laine Colbert needlepoint yarn as shown in the key
Caron Watercolors 033
16 x 16 in (40.5 x 40.5 cm) upholstery fabric for back
Matching sewing thread
10 in (25.5 cm) zipper (optional)
Pillow form, 14 in (35.5 cm) square
60 in (1.5 m) heavy twisted cord
2 large tassels

Use 1 strand of yarn over 1 thread of canvas.

1 Find the center of the design and, using tent stitch (see page 123), work out from this point following the chart. As tent stitch tends to distort canvas, it is advisable to use a frame.

2 When the main body of the design has been stitched, work over some of the stitches in the carnation buds in tent stitch, using Watercolors 033 space-dyed thread. This will give a speckled effect and add interest to the design.

3 If the finished piece is not quite straight when completed, you will need to block (damp stretch) it (see page 119).

Detail of Carnation Pillow.

4 Trim the canvas to within $^3/_4$ in (2 cm) of the embroidery, cutting across the corners diagonally to within $^1/_4$ in (5 mm) to reduce bulk.

5 Pin and baste the embroidery and backing fabric with right sides together, trimming backing fabric to size. Machine- or hand-stitch together, leaving an opening large enough on one side to insert the pillow form. Overcast or zigzag the seams to strengthen them.

6 If you have chosen to insert a zipper, add it at this stage. Alternatively, simply turn the pillow right side out, insert the pillow form, and close the opening with small invisible stitches.

7 Handsew the twisted cord to the edge of the pillow where the embroidery meets the backing fabric, using matching thread. Bind the edges of the cord with masking tape until you are ready to sew them to the pillow, and make sure that you stitch them down firmly, as they tend to unravel very quickly.

8 Finally, stitch one tassel securely to each top corner, as shown in the photograph.

VARIATIONS

■ Work the design in cross stitch on linen, omitting the background colors and finishing as a pillow as instructed above.

■ Use the all-over carnation pattern to cover a footstool or chair.

■ Work the tulip border in cross stitch and use to decorate household linen—sheets, pillowcases, napkins, etc.

Carnation Pillow and Glasses Case.

Carnation Pillow

Key DMC Laine Colbert

∴∴	7375 Dark burgundy
▶▶	7591 Antique blue
s s / s s	7322 Light blue
⊤⊤ / ⊤⊤	7223 Light pink
■■ / ■■	7217 Deep pink
□□ / □□	7266 Dull purple

Caron Watercolors 033 space-dyed thread (see
step 2 in instructions)

Carnation Glasses Case

*Worked in cross stitch on canvas, this vibrant design would
make a delightful gift. It uses the same chart as the Carnation Pillow, but
has a somewhat different look because of the alternative threads
that have been used. The petals of the flower are worked in a wonderfully
rich space-dyed thread, the bud and leaves in pearl cotton, and the
background in yarn. (See photograph on pages 48–49.)*

Design size: $3^1/_4$ x $6^1/_2$ in (8 x 16.5 cm)
Stitch count: 38 x 78

5 x 8 in (12.5 x 20.5 cm) beige 12-mesh canvas
DMC Laine Colbert needlepoint yarn 7372
Caron Watercolors 084 or DMC variegated floss
DMC pearl cotton (#5) 744
5 x 8 in (12.5 x 20.5 cm) maroon velvet for back
Matching sewing thread
8 x 8 in (20.5 x 20.5 cm) maroon cotton lining fabric
18 in (45.5 cm) narrow gold cord

*Use 1 strand of yarn over 1 thread of canvas.
Do not separate the Watercolors thread into
strands, but use it as it is supplied.*

1 Follow steps 1–5 for the Carnation Pillow
(see pages 47 and 49), but leave the top edge
completely open. Turn the case right side out,
then turn back the extra canvas at the top edge so
that the wrong sides are together, and baste.

2 Fold the lining in half widthwise and join
the side and bottom $^1/_2$ in (1 cm) seams.
Trim and then overcast or zigzag the seams. Insert
the lining into the case and fold under the top
edges. Stitch the lining to the case at the top edge
using small invisible stitches.

3 Sew the gold cord to the edge of the case
where the embroidery and backing meet,
using small stitches. Turn in neatly at the top edges.

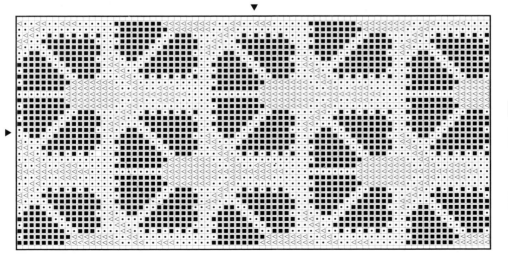

Carnation Glasses Case
Key   DMC
744 Pearl cotton (#5)

084 Watercolors from
the Caron collection or
DMC variegated
embroidery floss
7372 Laine Colbert

Heart Tree Birth Sampler

This delicately pretty birth sampler with hearts, flowers, tiny birds, bows, and a heart tree is sure to please. Worked in cross stitch and backstitch on linen, it will make the perfect gift for a new baby or small child.

Design size: 7 x 8 in (18 x 20.5 cm)
Stitch count: 98 x 114

11 x 12 in (28 x 30.5 cm) cream evenweave linen, 28 threads per inch (2.5 cm)
Embroidery floss as shown in the key

Use 2 strands of floss over 2 threads of linen.

Detail of Heart Tree.

1 Measure 2 in (5 cm) from the top of the fabric and 2 in (5 cm) in from the side and start working the top left-hand corner of the design at this point.

2 Work the cross stitches first, then add the backstitches.

3 Chart the chosen name and date from the alphabet and numerals given on pages 114–115 in pencil on graph paper, and position as shown on the chart.

4 Stretch, mount, and frame as desired (see pages 118–122).

VARIATIONS

■ Work the sampler in primary colors for a boy. This suggestion is made simply because most boys' rooms appear to be decorated in these colors as opposed to pastels.

■ Use a smaller backstitch alphabet (page 114) and include more information in the center heart, for example, weight, place of birth, and perhaps the parents' names.

■ Work just the center heart shape, the child's name, and the date of birth. Mount in a purchased greetings card, specially made for needlework, or make your own (see page 120), for a unique "welcome to baby" card.

■ Use the line of ducks to decorate a baby's bib, towel, crib sheet, bathrobe, etc.

Name

date

Heart Tree Birth Sampler

Key	DMC		
▣	818	Very pale pink	
▪	926	Light slate blue	
S	758	Pale apricot	
X	3348	Pale green	
⋮	828	Very pale blue	
▪▪	356	Apricot	

Work name/numerals in 355 Dark rust
Work the backstitch outlines in 924 Antique blue

Les Arbres

A plethora of trees adorn this unusual sampler. Worked in cross stitch on evenweave fabric, this delightfully simple design would suit a country kitchen perfectly.

Design size: 7 x 9¼ in (18 x 23.5 cm)
Stitch count: 125 x 162

11 x 13 in (28 x 33 cm) cream 18-count Davosa fabric
Embroidery floss as shown in the key

Use 2 strands of floss over 1 thread of fabric.

1 Find the center of the design and work out from this point following the chart.

2 Stretch, mount, and frame as desired (see pages 118–122).

VARIATIONS

■ Choose one line of the trees as a decorative edge for place mats or napkins.

■ Work the design on canvas (in cross stitch or tent stitch) and finish as a pillow.

■ Use any of the tree motifs separately for greeting cards.

■ Select any of the tree motifs to add to a sampler of your own design.

Les Arbres

Key	DMC	
■ ■	890	Dark green
S S	733	Light sage
\ \	470	Grass green
• •	434	Warm brown
I I	3371	Very dark brown
– –	581	Bright green
◄ ◄	632	Medium brown
▲ ▲	732	Dark sage
□ □	3051	Dull green
▽ ▽	831	Sage
▼ ▼	680	Dark gold

Fruit Tree

*This simple fruit tree motif, worked in cross stitch on linen,
shows that sampler motifs need not necessarily look traditional.
The addition of thread-wrapped cards as an inner mat
and decorative cords surrounding the outer mat lift
this piece out of the ordinary.*

Design size: $2^{1}/_{4}$ x $2^{7}/_{8}$ in (5.5 x 7.5 cm)
Stitch count: 31 x 39

5 x 5 in (12.5 x 12.5 cm) cream evenweave linen,
28 threads per inch (2.5 cm)
Embroidery floss as shown in the key

For the mat:
Piece of cardboard 8 x 8 in (20.5 x 20.5 cm)
4 pieces of cardboard $^{3}/_{4}$ x $5^{1}/_{2}$ in (2 x 14 cm)
1 skein DMC pearl cotton variegated 53
Glue/instant-bonding glue
24 in (61 cm) thick gold cord
60 in (1.5 m) fine navy blue cord

Use 2 strands of floss over 2 threads of linen.

1 Find the center of the design and work out from this point following the chart.

2 To mount the design, cut an opening 5 x 5 in (12.5 x 12.5 cm) in the center of the square cardboard to make a base for the mat.

3 Cover the narrow pieces of cardboard with the variegated thread by winding tightly around, securing the ends of the thread with glue.

4 Apply a line of glue along the side edges of the opening at the back of the cardboard base and press the two side pieces of the inner mat in place. Then glue the top and bottom pieces along those edges and let them dry.

5 Apply another line of glue approximately $^{1}/_{4}$ in (5 mm) away from the edges of the opening on the front of the gray mat and leave for one minute until the glue becomes tacky. Press the gold cord onto the glue, starting at the midpoint at the bottom. Trim so the ends just meet, and apply a little extra glue at this point to prevent fraying.

6 Apply another line of glue to the inside and outside edges of the gold cord, as close to it as possible. Adhere a length of navy cord to each side of the gold cord, following the instructions in the latter part of step 5.

7 Cut a 6 in (15 cm) length of navy blue cord and make into a bow. Glue the bow to the point where the ends of the cords meet.

VARIATIONS

■ Use this double mat in appropriate colors to frame any other suitable sampler motif in the book.

■ Add a border worked in the same two colors for a larger picture.

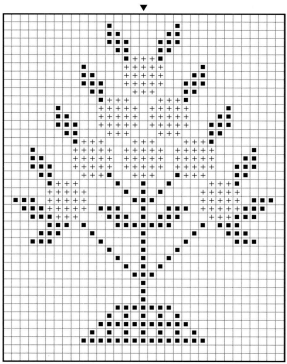

Fruit Tree

Key   DMC

413   Dark gray

680   Dark gold

Elizabethan Border Projects

This type of elaborate border worked in backstitch and queen stitch was very popular in Elizabethan times. Blackwork patterns were often used to decorate clothing—bodices, sleeves, gloves, and even shoes were covered in the most intricate embroidery. Because pattern books were rare and extremely hard to obtain, intricate patterns such as this would have been worked in bands on narrow strips of linen, now known as band samplers, not for the decorative purpose we now associate with the working of a sampler, but in the true sense of the word—as an example to work from.

The Bookmark
Design size: 2 1/4 x 8 1/2 in (5.5 x 21.5 cm)
Stitch count: 30 x 112

11 1/2 in (29 cm) unbleached linen band, 2 3/4 in (7 cm) wide, 30 threads per inch (2.5 cm)
DMC embroidery floss 823 Dark navy
DMC Gold thread D282
Matching sewing thread

Use 2 strands of floss over 2 threads of linen.

The bookmark is pictured on page 64.

THE BOOKMARK

1 Measure 1 1/2 in (3.8 cm) down from the top of the unbleached linen band and begin stitching the top middle "diamond," matching the midpoint on the chart to the midpoint of the linen band (widthwise).

2 Complete the design in backstitch and queen stitch (see page 123) following the chart.

3 When the embroidery is complete, turn under 1/2 in (1.5 cm) at the top edge and hem in position using matching thread.

4 Pull horizontal threads from the bottom edge to make a 3/4 in (1.5 cm) fringe.

5 Make two small tassels using embroidery floss and gold thread (see page 121). Position as shown in the photograph (see page 64) and attach with small stitches using gold thread.

The Checkbook Cover
The size given will fit a 3½ x 9 in (9 x 23 cm)
checkbook. Adjust the size as necessary to fit.

23 in (58.5 cm) white linen band, 4 in (10 cm) wide,
30 threads per inch (2.5 cm)
DMC embroidery floss 902 Dark maroon
DMC Gold thread D282
4 x 18½ in (10 x 47 cm) white iron-on interfacing
White sewing thread

Use 2 strands of floss over 2 threads of linen.

THE CHECKBOOK COVER

1 Follow steps 1 and 2 for the bookmark, but
begin stitching 2½ in (6.5 cm) from one end
of the linen band.

2 When the embroidery is complete, match
the center point of the iron-on interfacing,
with sticky side face down, to the center point of
the band, wrong sides together. Fuse by ironing.

3 Make a ½ in (12 mm) hem at each end of
the linen band, wrong sides together, and
hemstitch. Press hems.

4 Fold the hemmed ends back onto the stiff-
ened band with wrong sides together to make
a 2 in (5 cm) overlap. Overcast the top and bottom
edges of the folded ends so they form a pocket for
the checkbook cover to slip into. Press edges.

The checkbook cover is pictured on page 64.

VARIATIONS

■ Use this motif to decorate bed linen, either
worked on a linen band and stitched to the edge
of a pillowcase or sheet, or worked directly on the
bed linen using waste canvas.

■ This design would look wonderful as a pattern
for a belt, particularly if an antique buckle was
added.

■ Use the pattern to decorate a glasses case.

QUEEN
STITCH

Elizabethan Bookmark and Checkbook Cover
Key
Work the main body of the design in:
   DMC 823—Dark navy for the bookmark
   DMC 902—Dark maroon for the checkbook cover
Work details (shaded yellow) in Gold thread D282

Crowns Sampler

Although large numbers of crown and coronet patterns were used as decorative motifs on samplers, the original purpose of this pattern was for marking household linen. Noble households added coronets suited to their rank above their initials. It is unlikely, however, that all examples of this kind indicate noble rank; a far more likely explanation for the common occurrence of this motif is an affectation of the worker.
Worked in cross stitch, backstitch, and four-sided stitch on linen, this tiny sampler features eleven different crown and coronet motifs.

Design size: 4¹/₂ x 6¹/₂ in (11.5 x 16.5 cm)
Stitch count: 69 x 99

8 x 10 in (20.5 x 25.5 cm) cream Belfast linen,
32 threads per inch (2.5 cm)
Embroidery floss as shown in the key

Use 2 strands of floss over 2 threads of linen.

1 Find the center of the design and work out from this point following the chart.

2 Choose your own initials from the chart and work in four-sided stitch (see page 123). Add the date, using the numerals from the Band Sampler on page 16, charting out the details in pencil on graph paper.

3 Stretch, mount, and frame as desired (see pages 118–122).

VARIATIONS

■ Use one of the more elaborate crowns as a design for a pincushion.

■ For sheer affectation (unless you are of noble birth!), choose one of the crowns, add your initials underneath, and use to decorate your household linen. Use waste canvas (see page 122) if the fabric does not have an even weave.

■ Add any of these crowns or coronets to a sampler design of your own.

Crown Sampler

Key	DMC	
■ ■	924	Antique blue (work the border in four-sided stitch)
○ ○	502	Soft turquoise blue
+ +	680	Dark gold
S S	632	Medium brown
⋮ ⋮	3041	Mauve

Work lines of backstitch in 924 Antique blue

The Crowns Sampler is pictured on page 65.

"When This You See" Key Rack

This timely reminder should help to locate those "oh, so elusive" keys. Fun to make, this simple but effective design is sure to be either a perfect gift or a welcome addition to your home.

Design size: 3½ x 7 in (9 x 18 cm)
Stitch count: 49 x 97

7½ x 11 in (19 x 28 cm) 14-count gray Yorkshire Aida
Embroidery floss as shown in the key
Purchased sturdy wooden frame
Rounded hooks, as for cups

Use 2 strands of floss over 1 block of fabric.

1 Find the center of the design and work out from this point following the chart.

2 Stretch, mount, and frame as required (see pages 118–122). Make sure the frame you choose is sturdy enough to accommodate key hooks. Screw as many hooks as you wish into the bottom piece of the frame.

"When This You See" Key Rack
Key   DMC

▪▪ / ▪▪   924   Antique blue

×× / ××   300   Chocolate brown

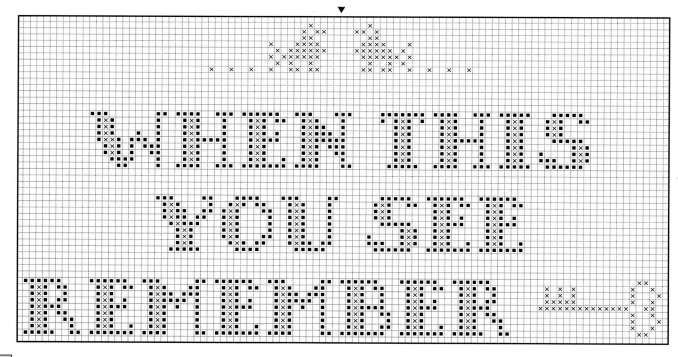

VARIATIONS

■ Replace the key motif with the word "me" for a traditional verse sampler. (You don't even need to chart the word for this, simply use the letters from "remember.") Substitute linen for Aida fabric and frame it traditionally for an authentic look.

The verse on which this design is based is as follows:

> *When I am dead and in my grave,*
> *And all my bones are rotten.*
> *When this you see, remember me,*
> *Lest I should be forgotten.*

Floral Border Pillowcase

Take a plain white pillowcase and transform it into a thing of beauty with this pretty floral border worked in cross stitch on linen. You could also use 4 in (10 cm) wide linen band, 28 threads per inch (2.5 cm), for this project, though it will make the border design a little bigger.

Pillowcase
Strip of white Belfast linen, 32 threads per inch (2.5 cm), 4 1/2 in (11.5 cm) x the width of your chosen pillowcase plus 4 in (10 cm) for allowances
Embroidery floss as shown in the key
Basting thread
White 2 in (5 cm) wide eyelet lace, twice the width of your pillowcase plus 4 in (10 cm)
for allowances
White sewing threads

Use 2 strands of floss over 2 threads of linen.

1 Measure 2 in (5 cm) from the bottom of the linen strip and begin stitching the border, matching the midpoint on the chart to the midpoint of the strip (widthwise).

2 Complete the border in cross stitch, working enough length to fit the width of your pillowcase. Trim along the short edge to within 1/2 in (1 cm) of the design.

3 Turn the long edges of the strip under 1/2 in (1 cm) with wrong sides together and baste in place.

4 Pin and baste the turned edges onto the eyelet lace, covering the raw edge, and at the same time, making small tucks in the lace at short intervals to give a slight fullness.

5 Turn under and baste the short edges of the linen strip. Finish the short ends of the lace with a narrow hem.

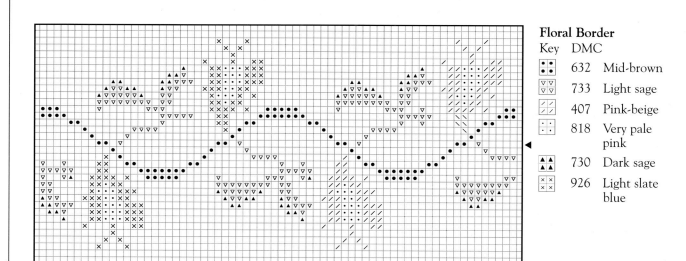

Floral Border

Key	DMC	
● ● / ● ●	632	Mid-brown
▽ ▽ / ▽ ▽	733	Light sage
⁄ ⁄ / ⁄ ⁄	407	Pink-beige
· · / · ·	818	Very pale pink
▲ ▲ / ▲ ▲	730	Dark sage
× × / × ×	926	Light slate blue

6 Position the linen strip with basted lace at the opening edge of the pillowcase and baste into position, being careful not to baste the pillowcase closed.

7 Machine- or hand-stitch the strip to the pillowcase at the edge of the linen. Remove basting stitches and press.

VARIATIONS

■ Use the same idea—that is, the border plus lace—to decorate a plain white sheet.

■ Work a short length of the border on a piece of linen band and make it into a potpourri sachet.

■ Work the border to decorate purchased towels with an Aida insert.

House on the Hill Sampler

This sampler, worked in cross stitch on linen, has a bold alphabet with a myriad of motifs. Stitch and enjoy it in its entirety or pick out several of the motifs to use in different ways. The projects on the following pages will give you some ideas, but, as you can see, the possibilities are endless.

Design size: 9¹/₂ x 18 in (24 x 45.5 cm)
Stitch count: 132 x 252

14 x 22 in (35.5 x 56 cm) cream evenweave linen, 28 threads per inch (2.5 cm)
Embroidery floss as shown in the key

Use 2 strands of floss over 2 threads of linen.

1 Find the center of the design and work out from this point following the chart.

2 Substitute your own name and the date by using any of the alphabets on pages 114–115 and the numerals from this chart.

3 Stretch, mount, and frame as desired (see pages 118–122).

House on the Hill
Key   DMC

	730	Sage green		738	Light beige		3041	Mauve
	310	Black		840	Dark brown			Ecru
	918	Medium rust		924	Antique blue		356	Apricot
	680	Dark gold		926	Light slate blue		407	Pink-beige

ADDITIONAL PROJECTS FROM THE HOUSE ON THE HILL SAMPLER

Shown here are examples that demonstrate how the House on the Hill chart can be used to create a wide variety of projects. This idea of extracting one or more motifs from a sampler and using them in a totally different way is really what this book is all about. Although these projects are wide ranging and varied, the possibilities are endless. You can apply the same idea to any of the samplers in the book, and of course to samplers in general. Take a *really* good look at all the component parts of a sampler; study them individually and carefully. Forget about size or color—both can be adapted; concentrate mainly on shape and composition; think about alternative fabrics and threads, and, finally, let your imagination run riot!

Birds and Flowers

Charming in its simplicity, this motif of small birds and flowers is worked in cross stitch on Rustico fabric. It would make an ideal introduction to cross stitch for a beginner.

Design size: $4^1/_2$ x $5^1/_4$ in (11.5 x 13.5 cm)
Stitch count: 62 x 71

$7^1/_2$ x $8^1/_4$ in (19 x 21 cm) 14-count Rustico fabric
Embroidery floss as shown in the key

Use 2 strands of floss over 1 block of fabric.

1 Find the center of the design and work out from this point following the chart.

2 Stretch, mount, and frame as desired (see pages 118–122).

VARIATIONS

■ Work the design in yarn on interlock canvas with 10 holes per inch (2.5 cm). Then add a simple border for a stylish sampler pillow.

■ Try working the whole motif in just one space-dyed or variegated thread. Add one or two harmonizing motifs and a matching frame.

Key	DMC	
	356	Apricot
	926	Light slate blue
	924	Antique blue
	680	Dark gold
	3371	Very dark brown

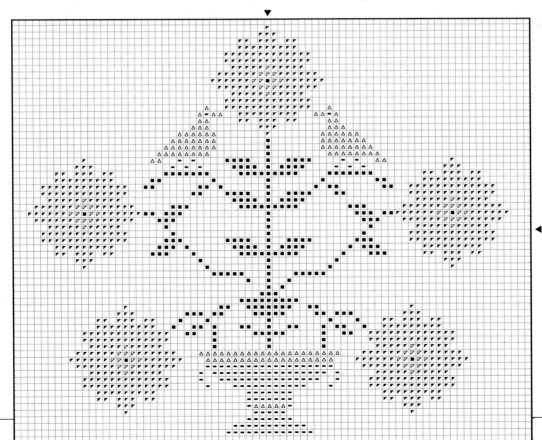

Yellow Birds Sampler

Tiny yellow birds worked in tent stitch on linen and outlined in backstitch adorn this sampler with its traditional border of chrysanthemums.
The main body of the sampler is worked in cross stitch. The initials are an unusual feature, in that they are worked in eyelet stitch with one thread of linen pulled from the edge of the ground fabric.

Design size: 8 x 8 in (20.5 x 20.5 cm)
Stitch count: 99 x 99

12 x 12 in (30.5 x 30.5 cm) natural Dublin linen, 25 threads per inch (2.5 cm)
Embroidery floss as shown in the key

Use 2 strands of floss over 2 threads of linen for the main body of the sampler, and over 1 thread of linen for the yellow birds.

1 Remove two threads from each side edge of the cut linen. These will be used to work your initials in eyelet stitch. Twelve-inch lengths (30.5 cm) are perfect for working in this medium as untwisted linen thread is apt to fray if longer lengths are used.

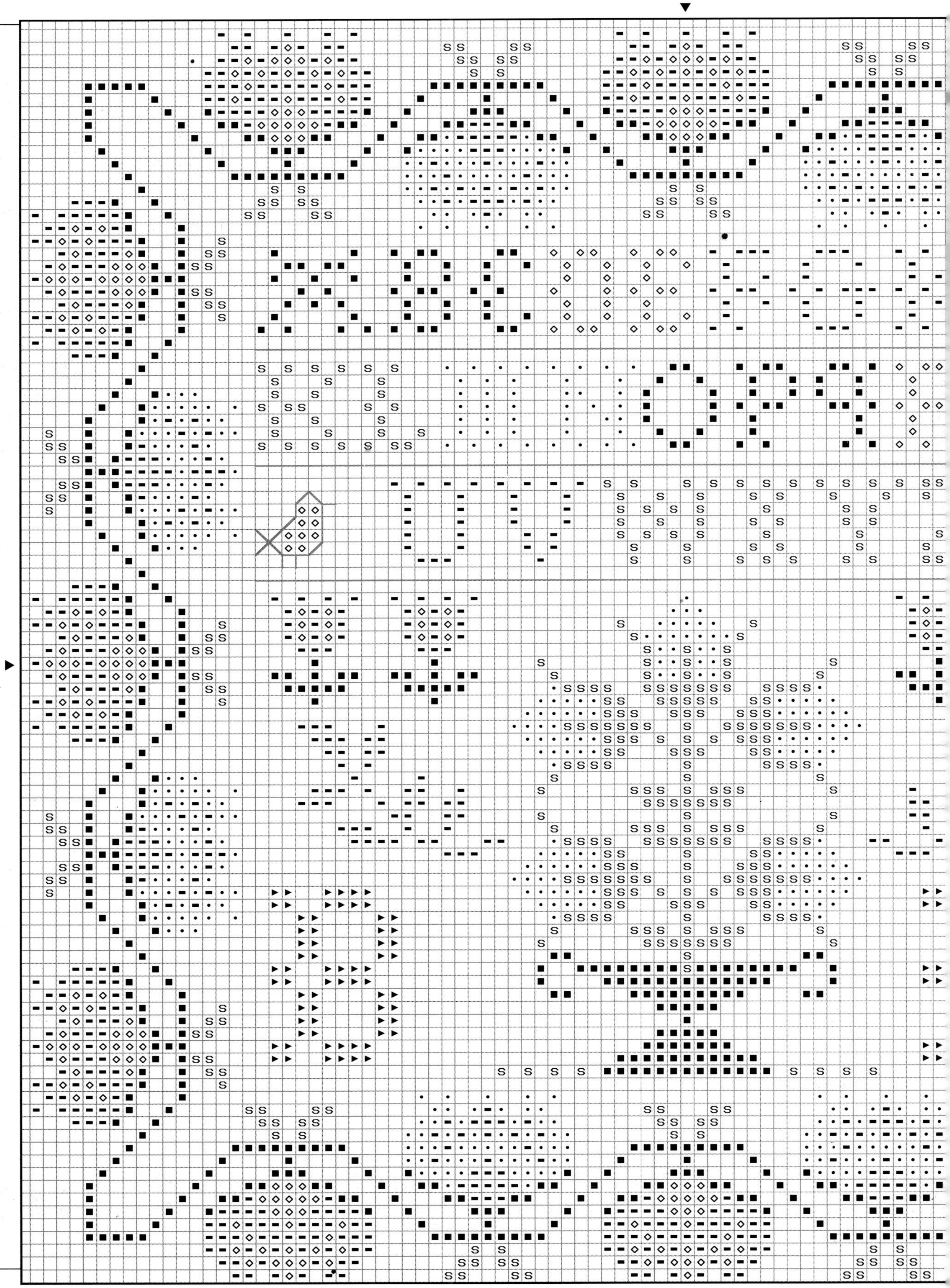

2 Find the center of the design and work out from this point following the chart.

3 Choose your initials from those given on the sampler and work in linen thread in eyelet stitch (see page 123) over two threads of linen. Each complete stitch will cover four by four threads, and therefore will be twice the size of the letters of the alphabet. Position as shown on the chart.

4 Stretch, mount, and frame as desired (see pages 118–122).

VARIATIONS

■ Elements from this design can be successfully used for other projects; the flowerpot motif, for example, could be used for a greeting card or to decorate a trinket box lid.

■ Use the small tulips as a continuous border to decorate household linen, such as towels and pillowcases, etc.

Yellow Bird Sampler

Key DMC

300 Chocolate brown

502 Soft turquoise blue

407 Pink-beige

745 Soft yellow

924 Antique blue

Use one thread of linen pulled from side edge (see step 1)

Note: The tiny birds are worked in with tent stitch (see page 123) in 745. Outline in backstitch with 300.

Flora and Fauna Box Lid

By far the most common motifs found on samplers, regardless of age or country, are plants and animals. This design shows a variety of flora and fauna, ranging from stags to birds, and tiny bushes to oversized trees. As is the norm in designs of this kind, scale does not exist. This design is worked entirely in cross stitch on very fine Edinburgh linen.

Design size: $6^{1}/_{2}$ x $8^{1}/_{2}$ in (16.5 x 21.5 cm)
Stitch count: 112 x 154

$10^{1}/_{2}$ x $12^{1}/_{2}$ in (26.5 x 31.5 cm) unbleached Edinburgh linen, 36 threads per inch (2.5 cm)
Embroidery floss as shown in the key
Wooden box with a lid designed so that an embroidery can be inserted, 7 x 9 in (18 x 23 cm)

Use 1 strand of floss over 2 threads of linen.

1 Find the center of the design and work out from this point following the chart.

2 Fit the embroidery into the box lid following the manufacturer's instructions.

VARIATIONS

■ This design would translate successfully to canvas for use either as a pillow or a stool top.

■ Many of the motifs could be used individually as designs for greeting cards, pincushions, etc.

■ Adding one or more alphabets at the top of the design and, perhaps, a border, this would make a stunning motif sampler, offering a real challenge to an experienced embroiderer.

Detail of Flora and Fauna motif.

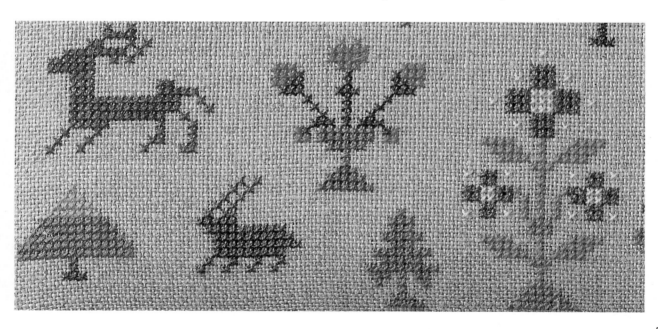

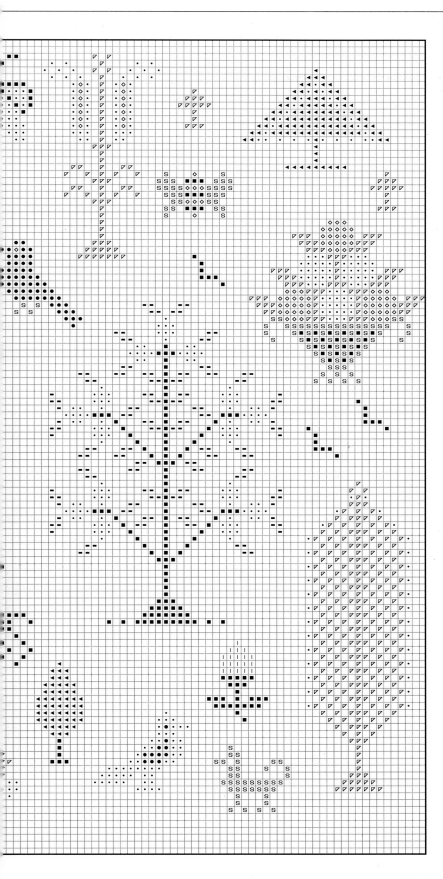

Flora and Fauna Box Lid

Key   DMC

■■	938	Dark brown
∶∶	355	Dark rust
◀◀	732	Sage green
SS	434	Warm brown
••	413	Dark gray
==	3051	Dull green
I I	733	Light sage green
◇◇	748	Very pale beige
▽▽	890	Dark green

Birds in a Bower

This pretty birds-in-a-bower motif is extremely versatile and can be used in a number of different ways. The two versions shown here present a strong contrast in their use of color.

"Silhouette" Birds in a Bower
Design size: $1^7/_8$ x $2^1/_8$ in (4.5 x 5.5 cm)
Stitch count: 58 x 65
5 x 5 in (12.5 x 12.5 cm) white Belfast linen, 32 threads per inch (2.5 cm)
DMC embroidery floss Black 310

Use 1 strand of floss over 1 thread of linen.

"Rustic" Birds in a Bower
Design size: $3^1/_4$ x $3^5/_8$ in (8 x 9 cm)
Stitch count: 58 x 65

$5^1/_2$ x 6 in (14 x 15 cm) 18-count Rustico fabric
Embroidery floss as shown in the key

Use 2 strands of floss over 1 block of fabric.

1 Find the center of the design and work out from this point following the chart.

2 Stretch, mount, and frame as desired (see page 118–122).

VARIATIONS

■ Use the design for a pincushion—worked in either yarn on canvas or embroidery floss on linen or Aida.

■ Add initials (choose from the alphabets that are given on pages 114–115) and make a greeting card. Use either a purchased card or make your own.

■ Use the design as a center panel for a pillow. This would look particularly striking worked in black on white and surrounded with black and white log cabin patchwork.

■ Work in pastel colors for a small wedding sampler. Add the bride's and groom's names or initials on the sides of the base, and the date underneath, using a small backstitch alphabet (see pages 114–115).

Birds in a Bower

Key	DMC				
■■	413	Dark gray	◇◇	926	Light slate blue
▲▲	356	Apricot	××	407	Pink-beige

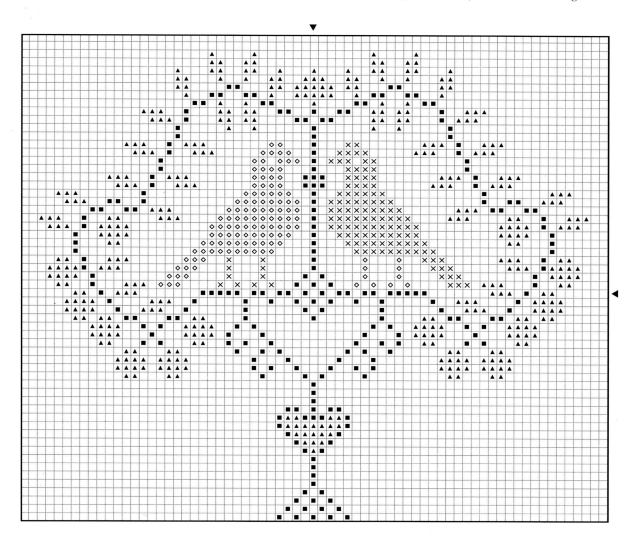

Blackwork Sampler

*Blackwork is sometimes referred to as Spanish work,
in the mistaken belief that it was Catherine of Aragon who introduced
it to England. In fact, she merely popularized a style of
embroidery that had been worked since the 15th century.
The outline stitch used, known as double running stitch, is referred
to as Holbein stitch, because it appears in so many paintings by
Hans Holbein depicting dress in the Tudor period. We have used
backstitch, which looks the same.*

Design size: 5 1/4 x 13 1/4 in (13.5 x 33.5 cm)
Stitch count: 66 x 164

*9 x 17 in (23 x 43 cm) cream Dublin linen, 25 threads
per inch (2.5 cm)*
DMC embroidery floss Black 310
DMC Gold thread D282

*See specific instructions on the chart for numbers
of threads to use.*

1 Find the center of the design and work out
from this point following the chart.

2 Choose your initials and numerals from those
given on pages 114–115. Chart the details

in pencil on graph paper and position as shown on
the chart.

3 Stretch, mount, and frame as desired (see
pages 118–122).

VARIATIONS

■ Choose any of the borders or patterns shown
and incorporate them into your own sampler.
Although it is called "blackwork," this type of
embroidery was frequently worked in red or blue
and looks just as effective in color.

■ The pattern just below the initials in the center
of the design would look stunning worked as a
border on white linen napkins. You could even
include your initials as shown for added impact.

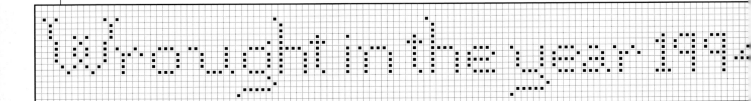

Wrought in the year 1994

Work diamonds with 1 strand, verticals with 3 strands

Use 1 strand

Use 2 strands

Use 2 strands

Gold cross stitch outlined with 2 strands

Use 2 strands

Use 3 strands

Use 2 strands

Use 1 strand

Use 2 strands

⊡ Cross stitch outlined with 2 strands

Use 1 strand

Use 3 strands for base line

Use 2 strands

Use 2 strands

Use 2 strands

■ Eyelet stitch over 4 threads in gold

Use 2 strands

Use 1 strand

Use 2 strands

Use 2 strands

Use 2 strands and fill in flower base with gold thread in tent stitch over 1 thread of linen

Use 2 strands

Use 1 strand

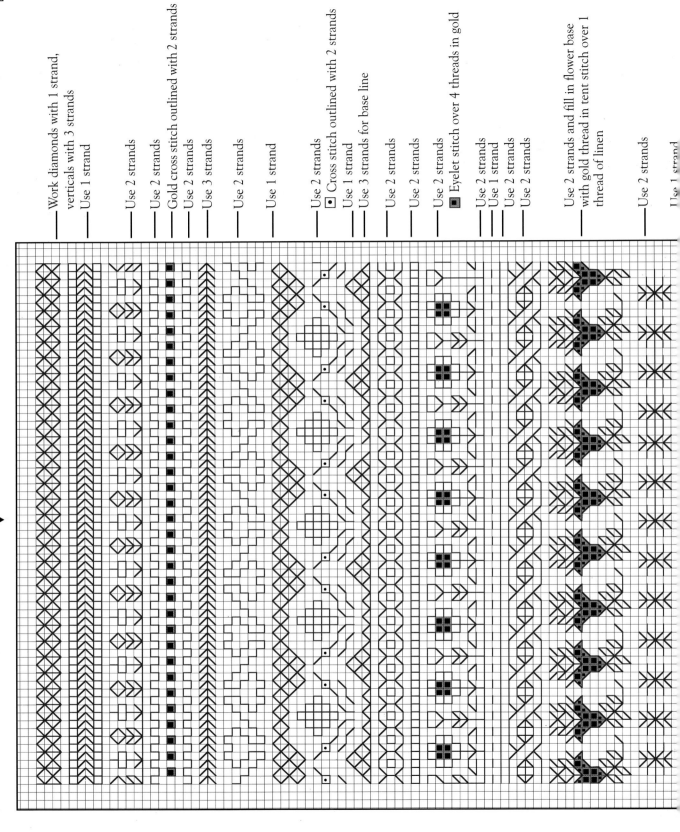

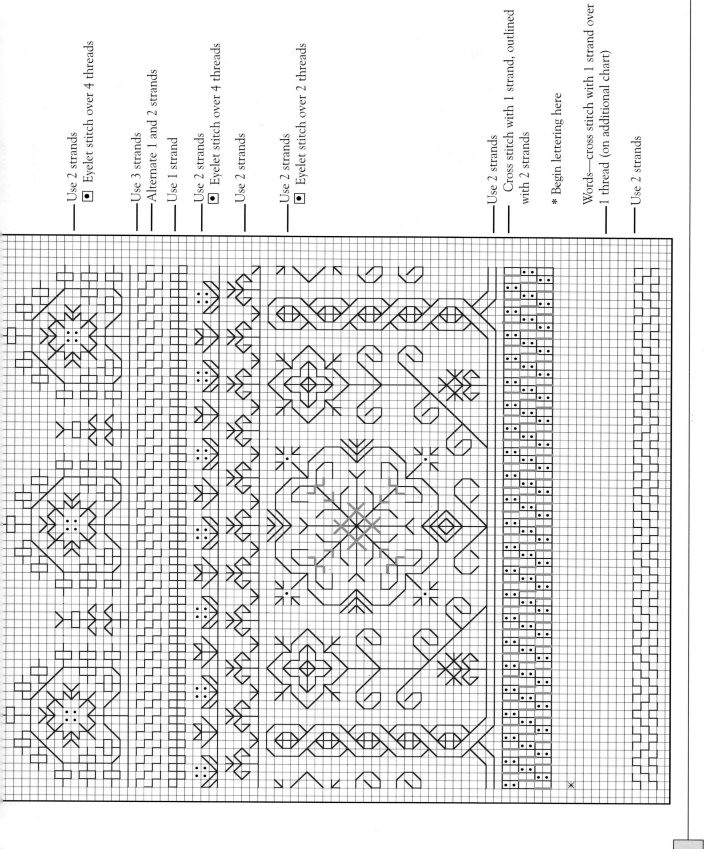

Use 2 strands
• Eyelet stitch over 4 threads

Use 3 strands
Alternate 1 and 2 strands

Use 1 strand

Use 2 strands
• Eyelet stitch over 4 threads

Use 2 strands

Use 2 strands
• Eyelet stitch over 2 threads

Use 2 strands

Cross stitch with 1 strand, outlined with 2 strands

* Begin lettering here

Words—cross stitch with 1 strand over 1 thread (on additional chart)

Use 2 strands

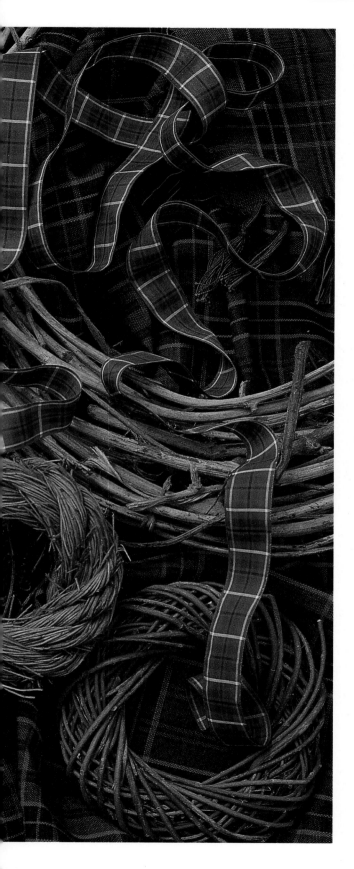

Victorian Alphabet

This simple Victorian alphabet design is worked in cross stitch on linen using space-dyed thread. Although this is a very modern thread, it certainly gives a very Victorian feel to the design.

Design size: $5^1/_2$ x $6^5/_8$ in (14 x 17 cm)
Stitch count: 77 x 93

$9^1/_2$ x $10^1/_2$ in (24 x 27 cm) cream 28-count Quaker cloth
Wildflowers, color Ruby, from the Caron collection

Use 1 strand of thread over 2 threads of linen.

1 Find the center of the design and work out from this point following the chart.

2 Stretch, mount, and frame as desired (see pages 118–122).

VARIATIONS

■ Using waste canvas (see page 122), use any of the letters of the alphabet to decorate items of clothing.

■ Replace the alphabet with a Victorian verse or motto, for example, "Improve thy time, Now in thy prime" or "Patience is a virtue," etc. Use one of the alphabets on pages 114–115 or see page 46 and pages 74–75.

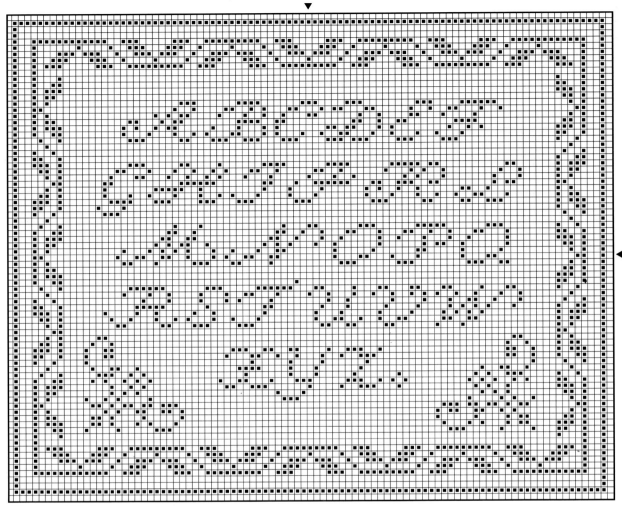

Victorian Alphabet.

Initialed Needlecase Lid Alphabet.

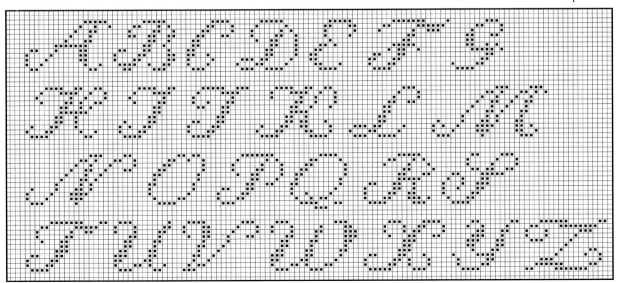

Initialed Needlecase Lid

Very Victorian in flavor, the design adorning the lid of this charming wooden needlecase (see photograph on page 98) is worked in tent stitch using variegated silk thread, although you could use embroidery floss if you prefer.

Design size: $1^3/_8$ x $2^3/_4$ in (7 x 3.5 cm)
Stitch count: 37 x 81

3 x 5 in (7.5 x 12.5 cm) cream Belfast linen,
32 threads per inch (2.5 cm)
Variegated silk thread in blue/gray/brown or use
DMC variegated embroidery floss 91 and 105, vary-
ing the lengths to achieve the effect shown
Wooden needlecase
Glue

Use 1 strand of variegated silk thread or 2 strands
of floss over 1 thread of linen.

1 Find the center of your chosen initial from the alphabet chart opposite and match to the center of the main chart. Mark the position lightly on the chart in pencil, then match to the center of the fabric. Begin work at this point and use a tent stitch (page 123) following the chart.

2 When the embroidery is complete, fit it into the needlecase lid, following the manufacturer's instructions.

3 Make a twisted cord (see page 121) using four lengths of the variegated silk or two lengths of floss. Trim to size and glue to the outside edge of the embroidered panel where it meets the wood, starting and finishing at the bottom midpoint.

VARIATIONS

■ Work the design in cross stitch over two threads of linen (this will double the size), trim the linen to an oval shape, allowing an inch (2.5 cm) around the design, and trim with lace to make a pretty table mat.

■ Use the initial design and border below to decorate an oval trinket box lid.

■ Use a single flower motif to add impact to an initial.

■ Using waste canvas (see page 122), use the design to decorate clothing—a pocket on a dress or blouse, or the front of a sweatshirt, for example.

Initialed Needlecase Lid Border.

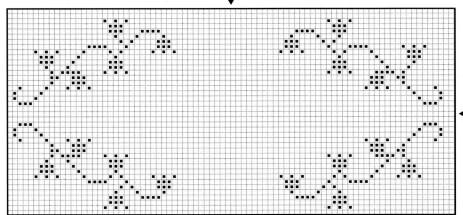

Strawberry Pincushion

A simple repeat motif of a strawberry adorns this easy-to-make pincushion. Worked in tent stitch with crewel yarn and embroidery floss on canvas, this decorative pincushion would make a wonderful gift for a friend who enjoys embroidery, or simply to use as a decorative piece in its own right.

Design size: 4³/₄ in (12 cm) diameter

7 x 7 in (18 x 18 cm) yellow 22-count petit point canvas
DMC Medici yarn and embroidery floss as shown in the key
4¹/₄ in (10 cm) wooden pincushion base

Use 1 strand of yarn, or 2 strands of floss where appropriate, over 1 thread of canvas.

1 Draw a 4³/₄ in (12 cm) circle in the center of the canvas using a felt-tip pen. As tent stitch tends to distort fabric, it is advisable to use a frame. Work out from the center of the circle.

2 Stitch the strawberry motif design in tent stitch (see page 123), working from the chart until the whole area has been covered. Use short lengths of yarn, since it frays very quickly, which will result in uneven coverage.

3 Remove the finished work from the frame and fit embroidery into the pincushion base, following the manufacturer's instructions.

VARIATIONS

■ Work the design as above, but increase the size of the circle and use for a footstool.

■ Work the design in cross stitch on a larger mesh canvas to make a pillow, repeating the motif until the desired size is achieved.

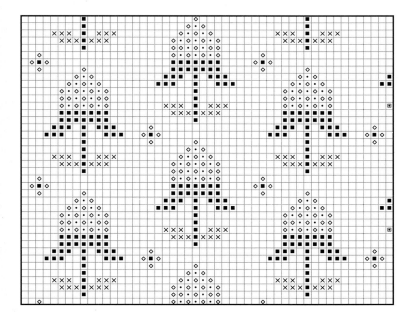

Strawberry Pincushion
(photograph on facing page)
Key   DMC Medici yarn
8100   Maroon
8403   Dark green
8401   Bright sage green
850   Beige (background)

DMC Embroidery floss
744   Pale yellow

House Picture

Houses such as this are much in evidence on samplers of the 18th and 19th centuries. Often the worker would portray her own house (or school, in some cases), thus recording it for posterity. This design, worked in tent stitch on linen, will afford you the same opportunity, whether you work the house shown and add your own house name, or number and street, etc., or chart a design of your own house (see page 122 for help and advice), and substitute it for the one shown.

Design size: $2\frac{1}{2}$ x $3\frac{1}{2}$ in (6.5 x 9 cm) with house name
Stitch count: 71 x 78 (without house name)

$5\frac{1}{2}$ x 7 in (14 x 18 cm) cream evenweave linen, 28 threads per inch (2.5 cm)
Embroidery floss as shown in the key

Use 2 strands of floss over 1 thread of linen.

1 Find the center of the design and, using tent stitch (see page 123), work out from this point following the chart. As tent stitch tends to distort fabric, it is advisable to use a frame.

2 Chart your own house name (or number and street, etc.) using the small backstitch alphabet and numerals on pages 114–115. Chart your details on graph paper in pencil and position as shown.

3 Stretch, mount, and frame as desired (see pages 118–122).

VARIATIONS

■ In place of the house name, substitute "Welcome to your new home." Either frame as a small picture or use as a design for a greeting card.

■ Double the size of the design by working in cross stitch over two threads of linen. Add not only your house name, but also your family details, such as names and birth dates, and a simple border. The design is then transformed into a very effective family record sampler.

■ Work the design in cross stitch with yarn on a large-mesh canvas and make a pillow. You could work the design on rug canvas using rug yarn or several lengths of worsted weight yarn to make a really large floor pillow.

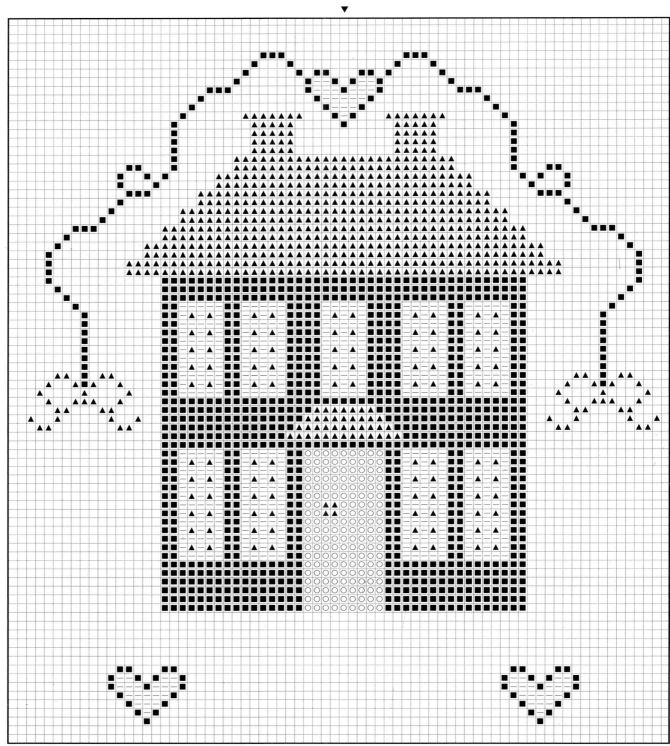

House Picture
Key   DMC

355   Dark rust

407   Pink-beige

322   Medium blue

356   Apricot

Bristol Orphanage Bookmark and Pincushion

The Bristol Orphanage samplers, made during the 19th century and consisting mainly of alphabets, numerals, narrow border patterns, and corner motifs, were worked in cross stitch using red silk thread on very closely woven linen. Many of these intricate samplers, showing strict economy of material, still survive, and serve as a reminder that embroidery was not always a labor of love. Girls as young as five would work one or more of these samplers as preparation for life as a household servant, with part of their duties being the marking of the home's linen.

The Bookmark
Design size: $1^3/_4$ x $6^1/_2$ in (4.5 x 16.5 cm)
Stitch count: 30 x 117

Purchased Aida bookmark
DMC embroidery floss Dull red 347

Use 2 strands of floss over 1 block of fabric.

The Pincushion
Design size: $3^1/_4$ x $3^1/_2$ in (8 x 9 cm)
Stitch count: 51 x 52

6 x 6 in (15 x 15 cm) white Belfast linen, 32 threads per inch (2.5 cm)
DMC embroidery floss Dull red 347
50 in (127 cm) white cotton lace, $2^1/_2$ in (6.5 cm) wide
White sewing thread
6 x 6 in (15 x 15 cm) white cotton backing fabric
Small amount of stuffing material

Use 2 strands of floss over 2 threads of linen.

THE BOOKMARK

1 Find the center point of the bookmark by folding fabric in half and half again. Match to the center of the design and work out from this point following the chart.

2 Choose initials from the alphabet charts on pages 114–115 and position as shown.

THE PINCUSHION

1 Find the center of the design and work out from this point following the chart.

2 Choose initials from the alphabet chart on pages 114–115 and position as shown.

3 Machine- or hand-stitch the two short ends of lace together and either overcast or zigzag to finish. Gather along the straight edge

Overleaf: Bristol Orphanage Pincushion and Bookmark.

103

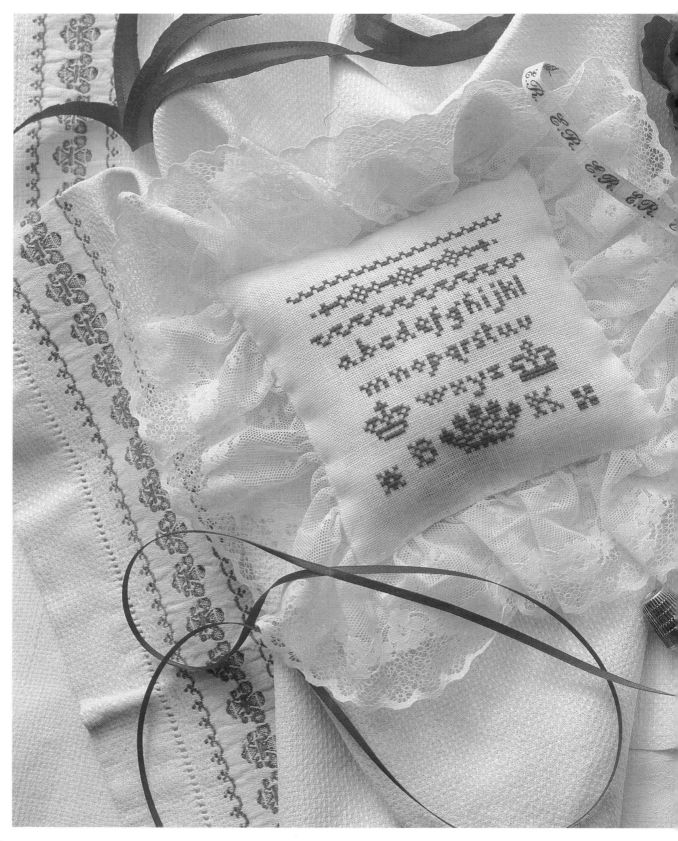

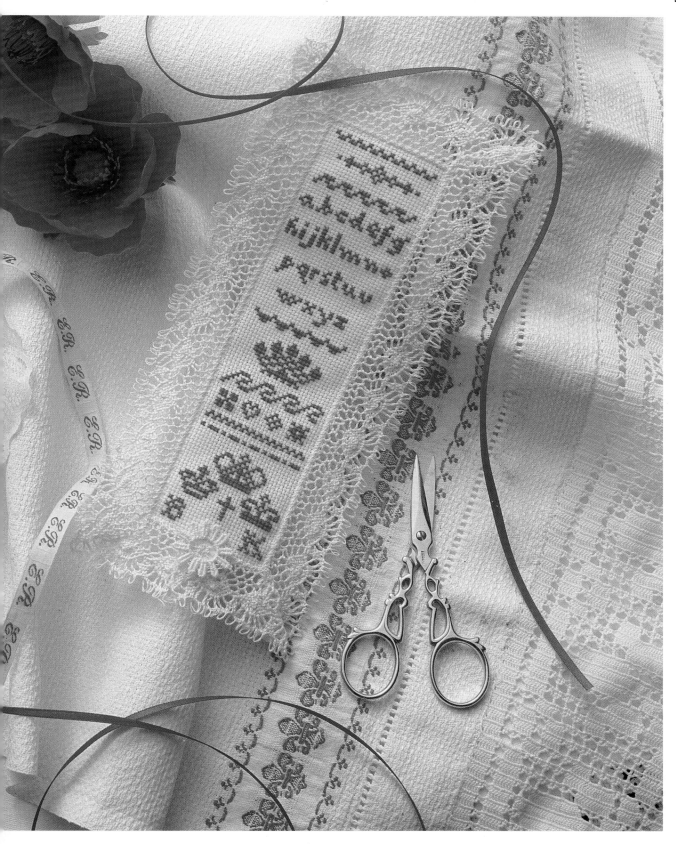

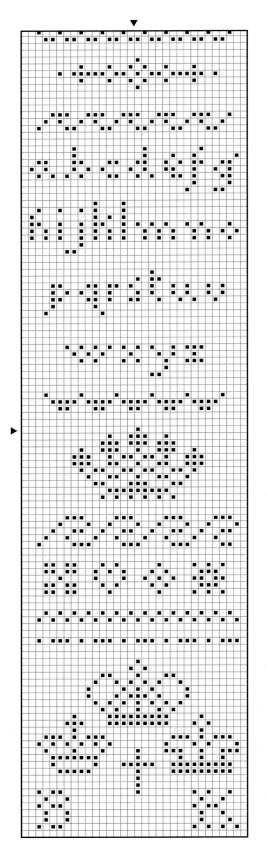

of the lace either by machine or hand, then pin and baste the gathered edge to the embroidered fabric, with right sides together, easing the gathers as you go.

4 Making sure that the ruffled edge of the lace is pointing toward the center of the work (you may want to baste this edge down so that it does not catch in the seam), place the backing fabric and embroidery right sides together, aligning the edges. Pin, baste, and then machine-stitch through all layers $\frac{1}{2}$ in (1.5 cm) from the edge, leaving a 2 in (5 cm) opening for turning right side out. Remove basting stitches.

5 Turn, stuff, then close the opening with invisible stitches.

VARIATIONS

■ Work the design as shown for the bookmark, mount on a velvet-covered card, and frame.

■ Work the pincushion design on fine linen and frame in a simple wooden frame as a charming miniature sampler.

■ Incorporate the alphabets, borders, and motifs into a larger, more complex design to emulate the Bristol Orphanage samplers of the past.

Bristol Orphanage Bookmark
Key   DMC
▦   347   Dull red

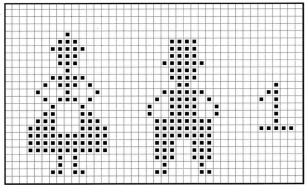

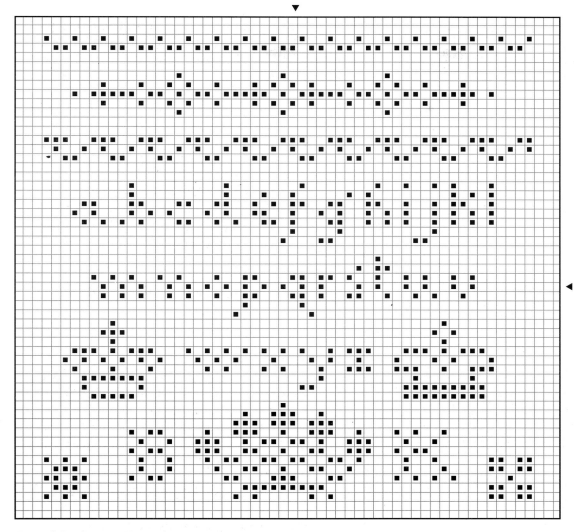

Bristol Orphanage Pincushion
Key   DMC
347   Dull red

Sampler Folk (chart for projects on pages 108–109)

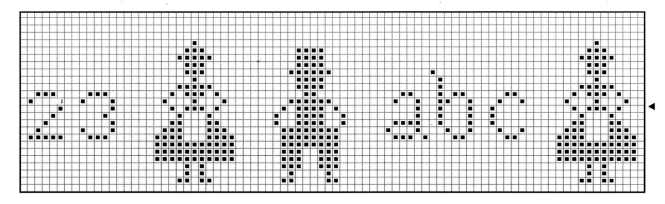

Sampler Folk

*Take the simplest of motifs—
a boy and a girl—add an ABC and
a 123, and you have the basis
for any number of charming
folk art designs. No sizes or specific
how-to instructions are given for
these projects, which range from a
shelf trim stitched on a purchased
linen band to a baby's drinking cup;
they are meant merely to inspire you.
By experimenting with a wide
variety of fabrics, threads, and ways
of display, you can use the
chart (on pages 106–107) to
create dozens of small projects that
can be completed quickly and
easily. All the projects shown
here are worked in cross stitch,
but you could, of course, work the
design in a variety of stitches,
which will further add to its
versatility.*

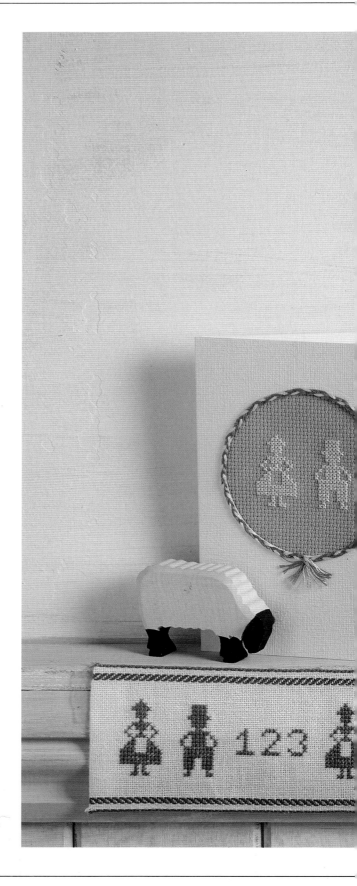

A Motif Sampler

This cross stitch sampler—a conglomeration of motifs, borders, and alphabets from the book—is really an example of what this book is all about. Why not try putting together your own sampler, a commemorative one, for example, in the same way? Or, if you do not feel experienced enough at this stage to tackle a complete design, try swapping and changing some motifs around and your finished sampler will be a piece that is unique to you. Confidence will be gained with practice, and by using the book in this way, you will be able to create unlimited designs of your own.

Design size: 8 ½ x 11 in (21 x 27.5 cm)
Stitch count: 107 x 137

14 ½ x 16 ¾ in (36 x 42.5 cm) unbleached Dublin linen, 25 threads per inch (2.5 cm)
Embroidery floss as shown in the key

Use 2 strands of floss over 2 threads of linen.

1 Find the center of the design and work out from this point following the chart.

2 Stretch, mount, and frame as desired (see pages 118–122)

VARIATIONS
■ Use any combination of motifs from this book to create a unique design.

■ Substitute the alphabet with names or a motto to personalize your sampler.

Key DMC

	730	Sage green
	500	Dark green
	434	Warm brown
	315	Plum
	918	Medium Rust

	738	Light beige
	407	Pink-beige
	926	Light slate blue
	3371	Very dark brown
	924	Antique blue

A selection of alphabets.

Traditional Symbolism of Sampler Motifs

Adam and Eve: *Good and evil*

Angels: *Martyrdom*

Apple: *Love/Fertility*

Bee: *Chastity/Virgin Mary*

Butterfly or moth: *Immortality/Resurrection*

Candle or candlestick: *Devotion/Prayer*

Carnation (pink): *Maternal love*

Cat: *Idleness*

Cherry: *Fruit of heaven*

Columbine: *The Holy Spirit*

Cross: *Faith*

Crown: *Hope/Eternity*

Crowned cross: *Eternity*

Daffodil or leek: *Wales*

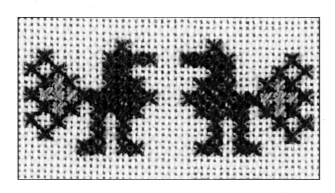

Dog: *Fidelity*

Dove: *Mercy/Peace*

Duck: *Marital fidelity*

Eagle: *Empire or, in Christian symbolism, the Ascension*

Falcon: *Pride/Nobility*

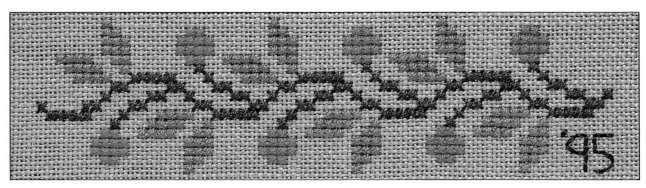

Garland: *Victory/Merit*
Goose: *Stupidity/Gullibility*
Hare: *Timidity*
Harp or lyre: *Purity/Music*
Heart: *Charity*
Honeysuckle: *Enduring faith*
Horse: *Fertility*
Lily: *Purity*
Lion: *Strength*
Marigold: *Obedience*
Monkey: *Laziness/Mischief*
Olive: *Peace/Goodwill*
Owl: *Wisdom*
Parrot: *Gossip*
Peacock: *Vanity*
Pelican: *Resurrection*
Pomegranate: *Hope/Eternal life*
Rabbit: *Gentleness*
Rooster: *Watchfulness/Penitence*
Rose: *Love/Patience/Beauty*

Shamrock: *Ireland*
Ship: *Journey*
Snake: *Reward/Wickedness*
Squirrel: *Mischief*
Stag: *Baptism/Gentleness and pride*
Stork: *Parental love/Bringer of happiness*
Strawberry: *Perfect righteousness*
Swan: *Love*
Thistle: *Scotland*
Tortoise: *Strength/Slowness*

Tree of Life: *Immortality*
Tulip: *Perfect love*
Unicorn: *Chastity/Purity*
Violet or daisy: *Humility/Modesty*
Weathervane: *Preacher*
Weeping willow: *Sorrow/Unhappiness*

Finishing Techniques

Before taking your embroidery to a professional framer or framing it yourself, it is advisable to run through the following checklist.

1 Always make a point of checking the completed design against the chart; it is very easy to miss stitches or even whole areas of a design.

2 Turn your work over and check for loose, trailing threads. Check that the threads are secure, then snip off as close to the work as possible. Dark-colored trailing threads in particular may show through light fabric and spoil the appearance of the finished work.

3 Unless your embroidery has become really grubby in the working, avoid washing and ironing it. Embroidery always looks better without this process. If you have taken the necessary steps to protect the work while in progress, have used an embroidery frame or hoop (one that is large enough to encompass not only the work but also to allow a reasonable margin for framing), and stored it—in a clean white pillowcase, for example—when not in use, then washing should not be necessary. If, however, it is necessary, wash by hand with mild soap flakes, taking great care not to rub or wring. Simply swish the embroidery around in the water. Rinse well, then roll in a clean white towel. Open out and let dry. To press, place several layers of towel on an ironing board. Lay the work face down on the towels, cover with a clean white cloth, and press with a warm iron. This method prevents the stitches from becoming flattened. Do not iron plastic canvas or perforated paper.

Stretching and Mounting Your Work

This part of the finishing process is vital because the most wonderful piece of work can be totally ruined if it is puckered or creased. It is always worth going to the trouble of finishing your work properly by stretching and mounting it (unless it is very tiny).

1 Use a strong, acid-free mat board (available from good art suppliers) or masonite covered with acid-free paper. Measure your work and cut the board slightly bigger than your embroidery if a mat is to be used; if not, cut to the size of your chosen frame.

2 Place the board on the wrong side of the embroidery and, when they are both in position,

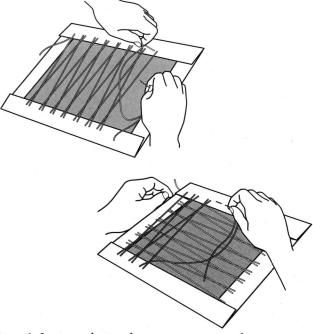

Figure 1: Lacing technique for mounting your work.

118

secure with straight pins inserted into one edge. Turn over frequently to check that the embroidery remains correctly placed.

3 Fold over the opposite edges of the fabric, then use a long length of strong thread (crochet cotton is ideal) to lace back and forth (Figure 1a). Pull the stitches up to tighten and secure firmly.

4 Complete the other two sides by lacing in the same way (Figure 1b).

Blocking Needlepoint

If you have not used a frame (or sometimes even if you have), needlepoint can become badly distorted and will need to be stretched back into shape. You will need a piece of thick wooden board larger than your embroidery (and soft enough to take thumbtacks), several sheets of newspaper or blotting paper, plain white porous paper on which you have drawn the outline of your embroidery in waterproof pen, and rustproof thumbtacks.

Lay the sheets of paper on the wooden board and wet them thoroughly; a plant mister is ideal for this purpose. Place the sheet of white paper with the outline of your design marked on it on top. Lay the embroidery, right side up, centered on top of this and, starting at top center, insert the thumbtacks at intervals of approximately 1 in (25 mm), working outward and stretching the canvas as you go. Pin along the bottom edge and then the sides in the same way. Let the canvas dry thoroughly—this could take as long as two or three days. If the canvas was badly distorted, it may be necessary to repeat the whole process.

Decorative Mats

Although traditionally samplers were framed without a cardboard mat surrounding the design (because they were primarily a functional piece of work), there is no reason why modern samplers have to follow the same pattern. Obviously, if you choose to work a very traditional design and you

want it to look authentic, then the addition of a mat would be inappropriate, but since your reasons for working a sampler probably have more to do with decoration than authenticity—and the print of the exercise is, after all, relaxation and enjoyment—you should feel free to enhance the design in any way you choose.

Fabric-covered Mats

The technique of covering a mat with fabric means that you need not restrict yourself to a plain, uninteresting mat that does not always do justice to your work. Virtually any color, pattern, or texture is possible with this method. You will need heavy cardboard, fabric, glue adhesive, a metal ruler, a scalpel or craft knife, and a cutting board or several layers of cardboard to protect the surface you are cutting on. If you are making a padded mat, you will also need one or two layers of batting.

Covering a Mat with Fabric

1 Measure the completed embroidery carefully and cut the mat and the opening to the size required. Round, oval, and, in particular, heart-shaped openings are very difficult to cut perfectly, and even though you are covering with fabric, uneven edges will show. Unless you are very skilled, it is best to ask a professional framer to cut these shapes for you.

2 Cut the fabric to the size of the mat plus allowances for folding back. The allowances will vary according to the size of the mat and the type of the fabric chosen (for example, because of its thickness, velvet will require a larger allowance than thin cotton). Always make sure that you align the mat with the straight grain of the fabric.

3 Place the fabric right side down and position the mat in the center. If you are making a padded mat, cut the padding to the same size as the mat and place it between the fabric and the cardboard. Snip off the corners of the fabric as shown by the dotted lines in Figure 2a (page 120).

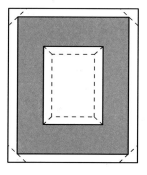 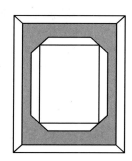

Figure 2: Covering a mat with fabric.

4 Apply glue to the remaining fabric at the outer edge. Fold over and press flat (Figure 2b).

5 To cut out the opening, first cut out the rectangle as shown by the dotted lines and then carefully snip into the corners, stopping just short of the edge. Apply glue to this remaining fabric, fold over, and press flat (Figure 2b).

6 Apply any further embellishments you would like to add—bows, sequins, braids, etc.—and then carefully align the mat over the embroidery. Secure it with glue or masking tape.

Framing

The choice of frame can make or break a piece of work. A relatively simple piece can be greatly enhanced or even transformed with a carefully chosen frame and/or mat. It is important, therefore, not to rush this process but to take some time to consider all the possibilities. You may have spent many hours on the work to be framed, so it would be sacrilege at this stage to spoil it with an inappropriate frame.

You need not go to great expense, however; often a coat of paint is all that is needed to transform a relatively dull frame. Choose colors that complement the worked piece. Small cans of paint available from hardware stores for trying out colors are an excellent choice; they are relatively inexpensive and will allow you to experiment by mixing colors to achieve the

desired shade. For a stippled effect, simply paint the frame in one color, then dip an old toothbrush in a contrasting color and run your finger along the bristles to flick the paint on to the frame (be sure to protect the surrounding area with plenty of newspaper). There are also many colored varnishes available that will greatly enhance a plain frame. Try matching one of them to the main color of your design.

Unless your work has a very raised surface or is very textured, the use of glass is advisable as it will protect the work from dust, dirt, and inquisitive fingers. Your framer will probably ask you to choose between plain or nonreflective glass. Nonreflective glass certainly sounds the obvious choice, but it has a rather mottled and flat appearance that tends to dull colors. Plain glass will show off your work to much better advantage. If you have decided to use glass but are not using a mat, ask the framer to use thin strips of cardboard, called spacers, to prevent the glass from coming into contact with your needlework. This will keep it from flattening your stitches.

Making a Folded Card

A variety of ready-made folded cards are now available from art and needlework shops. If, however, the size or color you want is not available, the following instructions will enable you to make your own.

1 Choose thin cardboard in a color to match your design.

2 Measure your embroidery to assess the size and shape of the opening. (Round, oval, and heart-shaped windows are much more difficult to cut accurately unless you have great skill.) Do not attempt to cut any opening with scissors; always use a craft knife.

3 Cut your card to the size and shape required (Figure 3a). Cut an opening in the middle section B and, using a craft knife, lightly score fold lines as indicated by the dotted lines.

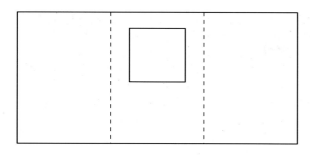

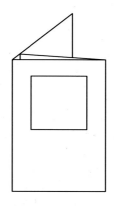

Figure 3: Making a folded card.

4 Position the opening over your embroidery. Trim away any excess fabric and glue your work in position or secure it with double-sided tape.

5 Fold A over B and glue together (Figure 3b).

How to Make a Tassel

1 Cut a piece of stiff cardboard to the length you wish the tassel to be. Wind the thread around the card until the required thickness is achieved. If you are making a set of tassels, keep count of the number of times you wind around the card so that all the tassels will be the same.

2 Thread a needle with a piece of the same color thread 3 to 4 times the length of the tassel. Pass it under the wound threads at the top, next to the card, and tie securely, leaving two trailing threads of the same length. Do not fasten off.

3 Cut the bound threads at the bottom of the card to release them.

4 Thread both of the ends used to tie the tassel into the needle, slide it through the top of the tassel, and bring out about $1/2$ in (1.5 cm) down (less for a smaller tassel).

5 Wind the thread tightly several times around the tassel to form the head. Knot securely and pass the needle back through the bound threads to the top. Use this remaining thread to attach the tassel to the article.

How to Make a Twisted Cord

1 Assess the length of cord required and cut a length of thread three times as long.

2 Make a loop in each end of the thread and attach one end to a hook or doorknob.

3 Slip a pencil through the loop on the other end and, keeping the thread taut, twist the pencil round and round until, when released, the thread begins to twist back on itself.

4 Keeping the thread taut, fold the length in half, matching the ends together. Stroke your fingers along the cord to even out the twists. Finally, tie the ends together. If a thicker cord is required, simply use more strands.

Charting Names and Dates

If you wish to personalize your work, for example, by adding a name and date, this is relatively easy to do. Chart the details in pencil on graph paper, adjusting the space to suit the letter chosen. For example, a lower-case "i" placed next to a lower-case "l" usually looks better with two spaces in between if the alphabet is very plain (even if only one space is allowed between the other letters). This type of adjustment will sometimes be necessary between other letters, but this will quickly become apparent during the charting process. When you have worked out your details, count the number of squares used vertically and horizontally, and position the lettering centered evenly and in the appropriate place on your fabric. You could also mark the position of your details lightly in pencil on the chart itself to make sure that they are correctly positioned.

Charting Your Own Designs

If you want to substitute a design (for example, your own house for the one shown in the House Picture, page 102), you can easily achieve this.

1 Take a good color photograph of the front of your home.

2 If necessary, enlarge the design on a photocopier to the size you wish the finished work to be. Many outlets now offer this facility.

3 Place a sheet of graph tracing paper over the design. This is available in various counts that correspond to the thread count of fabric, so if, for example, you wish to work on 14-count Aida,

choose 14-count graph tracing paper. Trace the design on the graph paper, squaring up the design and eliminating any unnecessary details.

4 Color the design using colored pencils or crayons. The chart is now ready to use.

Using Waste Canvas

Waste canvas can be successfully used to apply a charted design to nonevenweave fabric. Simply cut a piece of waste canvas slightly bigger than the overall finished design size and baste it into position on the right side of the chosen fabric or item of clothing.

Find the center of the charted design and match it to the center of the piece of canvas and fabric, then stitch. When completed, spray the whole design with water and, using tweezers, remove the soaked threads of the canvas one by one. Let the finished embroidery dry and press carefully on the wrong side.

Stitch Directory

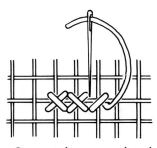

Cross stitch over one thread

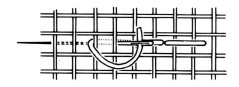

Backstitch

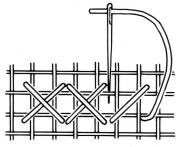

Cross stitch over two threads

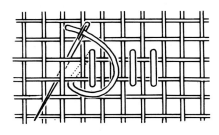

Satin stitch

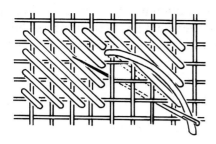

Reversed cushion stitch

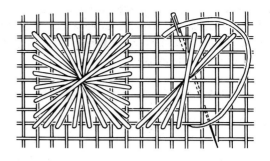

Rhodes stitch

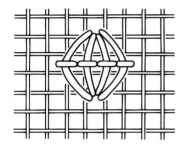

Queen stitch

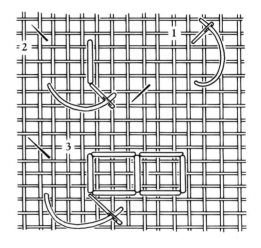

Four-sided stitch

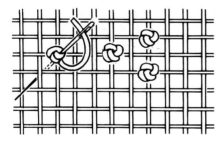

French knot

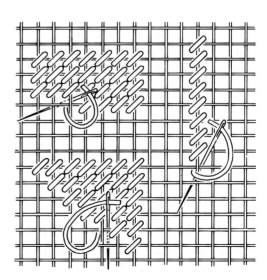

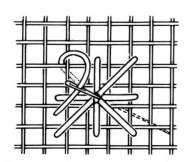

Eyelet stitch/Algerian eye

Tent stitch

Conversion Chart
Anchor shades in brackets indicate the nearest equivalent shade.

DMC	Anchor	DMC	Anchor	DMC	Anchor	DMC	Anchor	DMC	Anchor	DMC	Anchor	DMC	Anchor
Blanc	2	414	235	608	332	772	259	893	41	964	185	3364	(260)
Ecru	387	415	398	610	889	775	128	894	26	966	(206)	3371	382
208	111	420	374	611	898	776	24	895	1044	970	(316)	3607	87
209	109	422	943	612	832	778	968	898	360	971	316	3608	86
210	108	433	371	613	831	780	(310)	899	52	972	298	3609	85
211	342	434	310	632	936	781	309	900	333	973	297	3685	1028
221	897	435	1046	640	(903)	782	308	902	897	975	355	3687	68
223	895	436	1045	642	392	783	307	904	258	976	1001	3688	66
224	893	437	362	644	830	791	178	905	257	977	1002	3689	49
225	1026	444	290	645	273	792	941	906	256	986	246	3705	35
300	352	445	288	646	8581	793	176	907	255	987	244	3706	33
301	1049	451	233	647	1040	794	175	909	(923)	988	243	3708	31
304	1006	452	232	648	900	796	133	910	230	989	242	3712	1023
307	289	453	231	666	46	797	132	911	205	991	(189)	3713	1020
309	42	469	267	676	891	798	131	912	209	992	187	3716	25
310	403	470	267	677	886	799	136	913	204	993	186	3721	896
311	148	471	266	680	901	800	144	915	1029	995	410	3722	1027
312	979	472	(253)	699	923	801	359	917	89	996	433	3726	1018
315	1019	498	(1005)	700	228	806	(168)	918	341	3011	845	3727	1016
316	1017	500	683	701	227	807	168	919	340	3012	844	3731	(76)
317	400	501	878	702	226	809	130	920	1004	3013	842	3733	75
318	399	502	876	703	238	813	161	921	(884)	3021	905	3740	873
319	218	503	875	704	(256)	814	45	922	1003	3022	8581	3743	869
320	215	504	1042	712	926	815	43	924	851	3023	(899)	3746	1030
321	9046	517	162	718	88	816	1005	926	850	3024	397	3747	120
322	978	518	1039	720	326	817	13	927	848	3031	360	3750	1036
326	59	519	1038	721	324	818	23	928	274	3032	903	3752	1032
327	100	520	862	722	323	819	271	930	1035	3033	391	3753	1031
333	119	522	860	725	305	820	134	931	1034	3041	871	3755	140
334	977	523	859	726	295	822	390	932	1033	3042	870	3756	1037
335	38	524	858	727	293	823	(152)	934	862	3045	888	3760	(169)
336	150	535	1041	729	890	824	164	935	861	3046	887	3761	928
340	118	543	933	730	845	825	162	936	846	3047	852	3765	169
341	117	550	101	731	924	826	161	937	268	3051	861	3766	167
347	1025	552	99	732	281	827	160	938	381	3052	859	3768	779
349	13	553	98	733	280	828	9159	939	152	3053	858	3770	1009
350	(11)	554	(96)	734	279	829	906	943	188	3064	883	3772	1007
351	10	561	212	738	361	830	277	945	881	3072	(874)	3773	1008
352	9	562	210	739	366	831	(277)	946	332	3078	292	3774	778
353	6	563	208	740	316	832	907	947	330	3325	129	3776	1048
355	1014	564	206	741	304	833	(907)	948	1011	3326	36	3777	1015
356	5975	580	(281)	742	303	834	874	950	4146	3328	1024	3778	1013
367	217	581	280	743	302	838	380	951	1010	3340	329	3779	868
368	214	597	(168)	744	301	839	(360)	954	203	3341	328	3781	1050
369	1043	598	(167)	745	300	840	379	955	206	3345	268	3782	388
370	855	600	78	746	275	841	378	956	54	3346	267	3787	(393)
371	854	601	(63)	747	158	842	376	957	50	3347	266	3790	393
372	853	602	57	754	1012	844	1041	958	187	3348	264	3799	236
400	351	603	62	758	9575	869	944	959	186	3350	65		
402	1047	604	55	760	1022	890	(683)	961	76	3354	74		
407	914	605	(50)	761	1021	891	35	962	75	3362	263		
413	401	606	335	762	234	892	28	963	73	3363	262		

Bibliography

Cirker, Blanche (ed.), *Needlework Alphabets and Designs*, Dover (1975)

Clabburn, Pamela, *The Needleworker's Dictionary*, Macmillan (1976)

Colby, Averil, *Samplers*, Batsford (1964)

Crawford, Heather M., *Needlework Samplers of Northern Ireland*, Allingham Publishing (1989)

Deforges, Regine, and Genevieve Dormann, *Alphabets*, Albin Mitchel (1987)

Don, Sarah, *Traditional Samplers*, David & Charles (1986)

Edmonds, Mary Jaene, *Samplers and Samplermakers (An American Schoolgirl Art 1700-1850)*, Rizzoli International Publications, Inc. (1991)

Eirwen Jones, Mary, *British Samplers*, Batsford (1948)

The Embroiderers' Guild Practical Library, *Making Samplers*, David & Charles (1993)

Fawdry, Marguerite, and Deborah Brown, *The Book of Samplers*, Lutterworth Press (1980)

Forstner, Regina, *Traditional Samplers*, Rosenheimer Verlaghaus Alfred Forg GmbH & Co. (1983)

Hersh, Tandy and Charles, *Samplers of the Pennsylvania Germans*, The Pennsylvania German Society (1991)

Huish, Marcus, *Samplers and Tapestry Embroideries*, Dover (1970)

Kay, Dorothea, *Sew a Sampler*, A&C Black Ltd. (1979)

Lammer, Jutta, *Making Samplers (New & Traditional Designs)*, Sterling Publishing Co. Inc. (1984)

Lewis, Felicity, *Needlepoint Samplers*, Studio Vista (1981)

Meulenbelt-Nieuwburg, Albarta, *Embroidery Motifs from Dutch Samplers*, Batsford (1974)

Pesel, Louisa F., *Historical Designs for Embroidery*, Dover (1970)

Ring, Betty, *American Needlework Treasures*, E.P. Dutton (1987)

Ring, Betty, "American Samplers and Pictorial Needlework, 1650-1850" *Girlhood Embroidery* (vols. I & II), Alfred A. Knopf, Inc. (1993)

Ryan, Patricia, and Allen D. Bragdon, *Historic Samplers*, Bulfinch Press (1992)

Sebba, Anne, *Samplers: Five Centuries of a Gentle Craft*, Thames & Hudson (1979)

Snook, Barbara, *English Embroidery*, Mills & Boon Ltd., London (1960)

Stanwood Bolton, Ethel, and Eva Johnson Coe, *American Samplers*, Dover (1973)

Stevens, Christine, *Samplers (From the Welsh Folk Museum Collection)*, Gomer Press (1991)

Swain, Margaret, *Scottish Embroidery*, Batsford (1986)

Acknowledgments

My grateful thanks to the following people for all their help and support:
First and foremost, my wonderfully supportive husband, Chris, for always being such a
calming influence (sometimes so calm he seems almost unconscious compared to my harassed self).
My children, Katie and Nicholas—Katie for her wealth of good ideas for project variations,
and Nicholas for preparing the computer charts (when he would much rather be
playing rugby or supporting British Telecom with his excessive use).
My wonderful mother-in-law, Irene, and father-in-law, Jim, without whose constant help
and support everything would most certainly grind to a halt.
My agent, Doreen Montgomery, for all her ongoing help and encouragement.
Everyone at David & Charles for putting everything together so well, and Di Lewis for her
wonderful photography. DMC Creative World for fabric, threads, and the linen band for
the guitar strap. Mike Grey at Framecraft Miniatures for trinket boxes, bookmarks,
jar covers, and the wooden needlecase. Jane Greenoff for linen band and perforated paper.

More Information

For more information about threads please contact the following:

Anchor threads, Coats & Clark, 30 Patewood Drive, Suite 351, Greenville, SC 29615.

DMC threads and fabrics, DMC Corporation, Port Kearny, Bldg. 10, South Kearny, NJ 07032—
DMC threads, Zweigart fabrics

Brenda Keyes's sampler charts, complete kits, linen, needlework
accessories, and Country Yarns Thread Organisers are available from her company,
Country Yarns the Sampler Company, Holly Tree House, Lichfield Drive,
Prestwich, Manchester M25 0HX, England. U.S. readers can write for details or
telephone/fax 011 44 161 773 9330.

Index